AFTER WHITENESS

THEOLOGICAL EDUCATION BETWEEN THE TIMES

Ted A. Smith, series editor

Theological Education between the Times gathers diverse groups of people for critical, theological conversations about the meanings and purposes of theological education in a time of deep change. The project is funded by the Lilly Endowment Inc.

Willie James Jennings
After Whiteness: An Education in Belonging

Chloe T. Sun
Attempt Great Things for God: Theological Education in Diaspora

Amos Yong
Renewing the Church by the Spirit: Theological Education after Pentecost

AFTER WHITENESS

An Education in Belonging

Willie James Jennings

WILLIAM B. EERDMANS PUBLISHING COMPANY
GRAND RAPIDS, MICHIGAN

Wm. B. Eerdmans Publishing Co.
4035 Park East Court SE, Grand Rapids, Michigan 49546
www.eerdmans.com

Published 2020
Printed in the United States of America

26 25 24 23 22 21 20   1 2 3 4 5 6 7

ISBN 978-0-8028-7844-1

Library of Congress Cataloging-in-Publication Data

Names: Jennings, Willie James, 1961– author.
Title: After whiteness : an education in belonging / Willie James
    Jennings.
Description: Grand Rapids, Michigan : William B. Eerdmans Publish-
    ing Company, 2020. | Series: Theological education between the
    times | Includes bibliographical references. | Summary: "A multi-
    modal reflection on the way theological education can foster
    pluralistic community and resist Western ideals of individualism,
    masculinity, and whiteness"—Provided by publisher.
Identifiers: LCCN 2020020639 | ISBN 9780802878441 (paperback)
Subjects: LCSH: Theology—Study and teaching.
Classification: LCC BV4020 .J46 2020 | DDC 230.071/1—dc23
LC record available at https://lccn.loc.gov/2020020639

*This book is dedicated to
those who are in search
of a place to fill out that
Holy dream of a new world
down to the details of a life.*

Contents

Acknowledgments

I was waiting for a more opportune time to write this book, sometime after my next book was finished, but Ted Smith approached me about the Theological Education between the Times project and convinced me that this was the right time to write this book. He was right, and I am forever in his debt for drawing me into this wonderful work and into the lives of a fabulous group of scholars and teachers. Amos Yong, Chloe Sun, Daniel Aleshire, Mark Jordan, Elizabeth Conde-Frazier, Colleen Mary Mallon, Keri Day, Maria Liu Wong, Rachelle Green, Hoffman Ospino, Mark Young, and Uli Guthrie all helped me clarify my thinking and confirmed for me the urgency of this book and of all the books that will be published in this series. Ted Smith led us beautifully in this work with gracious wisdom, deep humility, and an extravagant hospitality that extended from our meals to our ideas. This book is inspired by the witness of Katie Geneva Cannon, William Pannell, Cheryl Sanders, Fumitaka Matsuoka, M. Shawn Copeland, Eleazar S. Fernandez, Daisy Machado, Vine Deloria Jr., Evelyn Parker, and Kwok Pui-lan. Along with being accomplished scholars, these wonderful souls saw deeply into the dilemmas I articulate in this book. I have learned much from their faithful efforts to mark a path forward. I am also thankful for my many years of consulting work for the Wabash Center for Teaching and Learning in Religion and Theology, under the leadership during my time of first Lucinda Huffaker, then Dena Pence, and now Nancy Lynne Westfield. Working with these brilliant directors along with Timothy Lake, Tom Pearson, and especially Paul Myhre allowed me the greatest gift a scholar and teacher could ask for—friends who saw the problems and the possibilities of theological education like I was seeing them. I am also very thankful for my work with the Association of Theological Schools, then under the leadership of Dan Aleshire and now under Frank Yamada. Consulting for these two crucial organizations allowed me to be with faculty, staff, students, and administrators from Vancouver to Florida, from Montreal to San Diego, learning about the intricate realities of this work of theological education. I also enjoy the great blessing of being able to teach and do my research at Yale Divinity School alongside a fabulous group of supportive colleagues, starting with our dean, Gregory Sterling. Words cannot capture my thankfulness for their friendship. I want to offer special thanks to my former colleagues at Duke University Divinity School for their unwavering love. We share what can only come through decades of life together—a deep understanding of our shared joy, anguish, and hope. I also live thankful each day for the world I share with Joanne Browne Jennings and our grown daughters, Njeri Jennings and Safiya Jennings. Everything I write lives near my thoughts of them and inside my gratefulness for their love and encouragement.

Prologue: Secrets

I was an academic dean at a divinity school. I learned the secrets. I cannot tell you the secrets, but I can tell you what they mean.

The secrets are mundane, as are all secrets, but what they mean speaks of weighty matters—of life and death and the power of tongues, of awesome hope and of great sorrow, and of bodies, many bodies, touching God and being touched by God. Then there is the fear, like a tide flowing in and out, colliding with joy, like strong waves hitting rocks and the mixture of joy and fear splashing over everyone, soft drops and hard bits of rock.

How was it that I as an academic dean came to know the secrets and their meaning? That question is within the larger question of how I as a black man in America came to be an academic dean of an overwhelmingly white divinity school in a major university in America.

.   .   .

I have always been a listener of bodies and a reader of thoughts. This fact is more and less mystical than it sounds. I have always loved books and the sensual act of reading—rubbing my hands across a page, delighting in the way letters dance on a page, sensing my breathing in and out as I connect the words and then the sentences and the paragraphs. And as they connect, I hear the voice the writer has created. Then and there the thoughts appear, open and free for anyone with the patience to see. Reading thoughts has always been a precious freedom for me.

I learned very early, however, through trial and error, that the voice formed as one reads the pages of a text is a phantasm, its connection to the actual author always a matter for speculation, and that how that voice connects to my thoughts and my voice is integral to that speculation.

Trial and error began for me when I too quickly imagined that the funny, irritating, maddening, wise, righteous, audaciously courageous or insightful voices I heard through texts matched authors who would see me, a black man, as their conversation partner. My many teachers disabused me early and often of that hopeful connection. "Pull the ideas forward, not the people," they said. All my teachers invited me into the work that would become my life.

I work in the fragments.

I learned to listen to bodies. It was a matter of survival. At home, I was the smallest child in a family of bigger people. At school, and in the neighborhood, I was the quiet, shy, sensitive boy surrounded by an exquisite variety of bullies, each a prodigy in their particular art of torture. In my town, white people (immigrants made white) ruled and exercised power in ways so ubiquitous that even they did not understand its extent, but their ignorance of their own power would be no excuse for my ignorance. I had to know how to listen especially to white people's bodies—their moods and manners, their joys and sorrows, and the slightest, almost imperceptible beginnings of irritation or anger or fear—because my life depended on it.

My well-being has always been inextricably bound to my racial senses, and still is, even now.

Listening to bodies and reading thoughts are only half the story of how I came to be an academic dean of a divinity school. The full story is God. I am a lover of God. It has been so since the beginning—since the womb of Mary, the lover of God. My mother, Mary, fed me Jesus in and with her milk, and in every meal drenched in the rich foods of the South. The smells, sounds, and tastes are so deeply part of my body that they are always with me, bursting through my memories into my present sensing and feeling. I live every day at the table Mary set for me.

The move from being a lover of God to a thinker about God was a very short first step in my journey, and it is a journey I am yet on. Academic life in the theological academy suited me because there, as a lover of God, I could nest inside my love of books and reading and thoughts freely flowing around me. But I could also have some semblance of control over whose bodies I would have to listen to, maybe even find some escape from having to listen to bodies that could do me harm.

Escape: It is a crucial element in my entering the academic life, but not mine alone. It is one of the secrets hiding in plain sight in higher education and especially theological education—in divinity schools, seminaries, theological colleges, and Bible training schools of all sorts. People often come to escape. People often end up teaching in order to escape.

Escape means so much.

Out of high school, I wanted to work at General Motors on the factory floor, just like my dad. Back in the late seventies and early eighties, one could make a lifetime with a job at GM. The kids I knew who got in were paid big for the time. My dad did not want me in GM, on the factory floor with him. The floor was big, loud, nasty, rough, barbarian. But I was shy, slight, effeminate; to his mind, I was a Sunday school boy not ready for a man's Monday. I self-inflicted my way through jobs the men in my life imagined would make me a man—electrician apprentice, grave digger, third-shift store clerk, UPS worker—hating each one. Then I failed into college, back-doored my way into junior college and then a liberal arts school, and the escape was on, my own personal underground railroad.

The most important thing I learned early in my journey was that I loved student life and teaching, to see it done well and later to do it myself. I remember the first time I heard a professor open class with a prayer. (I graduated from a Christian college.) After he prayed, he proceeded to quote Kierkegaard, Dostoevsky, and then Calvin. I felt as though I was walking through doors that had been placed on impenetrable walls and into hidden spaces revealed for the first time, although they were not quite safe spaces. Yet, in that preliminary moment of a class and a lecture, I felt the Spirit.

I spied a freedom in the academy that was not easily definable, but it was there. I sensed it. It was a freedom that said to me that I don't have to prove, show, demonstrate, acknowledge, or claim my being in any particular way that denies my being. This freedom shattered my blackness and my Christianity into little pieces. These little pieces were everything—thoughts, ideas, stories, laughter, tears, poems, gestures, sweat and dance, and so much more. Now I could play with them. Hold them loosely or tightly.

I work in the fragments.

This is how I came to be in the academy and came to be an academic dean, because I was a listener of bodies and a reader of thoughts. But I listened and heard more than what was being said. I paid attention and saw more than what was being presented.

I opened myself to institutional life, allowing my senses and my feelings to be carried by the emotional and intellectual currents that flow through a school, morning to night. All academic deans know this, but not all of us will do this. I did this as a young African American man serving in a predominately white divinity school woven inside a major research university. It remains a rare thing for someone like me to have served in this role in a theological educational institution in the United States.

.   .   .

To be an academic dean is to hold a unique place in the ecology of a theological school. We are the people who live in the middle, between deans (or presidents or principals, as they are called in different educational contexts) and faculty, and between faculty and students, and between staff members and faculty. Our work begins by interpreting to one the words, actions, and needs of the other, always trying to convey concerns both strong and weak in their best light. An academic dean moves and breathes down inside the educational processes of a school, trying to help facilitate the unique dance that is educating people. Like a director with script in hand and scenes in mind, we guide our colleagues in their performances of a curriculum that together we hope will yield a beautiful performance of a student that will linger for a lifetime. We aim at a performance that will be seen and experienced as formation.

Formation. Formation. Formation.

This is the most important word that I will consider in this book. Formation is an elusive thing to see in practice. It is the shining goal of all education, especially theological education. Few people in the world see it as an academic dean sees it, as I saw it. Watching a person enter a school, seeing who they are, what they think, where they focus attention at the beginning of it all, and then to behold who they are, what they think, and where they focus attention at the end of their program is remarkable, even spiritual.

Education and theological education kill the lie that people don't change. Formation happens, people do change, even if that change is not easily perceived by impatient eyes. I have seen many kinds of formation, many befores and many afters, among undergraduates, graduate students, and doctoral students. Even newly minted scholars becoming new faculty members and moving from the early years of teaching to the mature years to the senior season participate in a formation process.

I have learned, however, that the formation that attends theological education and, more broadly, Western education is troubled—in fact, deeply distorted. More than twenty-nine years of teaching, almost ten years as an academic dean, as well as many years of being a consultant to many schools on a variety of issues and advising a host of doctoral students and faculty members of schools across the country have only confirmed the distortion I witnessed as an academic dean.

Distorted formation has been with Western education for centuries, and now we have entered a moment when we might begin to address it. In fact, my goal in this extended essay is to point theological education toward a future beyond distorted formation. Even more ambitiously, I want to suggest that theological education carries the resources necessary to reframe Western education beyond that distortion. Such a direction for the future, I believe, is urgently needed not only for theological education but also for Western education. I am not intending to take on the restructuring of Western education in this work. But I do want to suggest to all educators an orientation toward formation worth considering.

Theological education in the Western world is shifting dramatically. Many schools are closing, enrollments are declining, degree programs at existing schools are metamorphosing into new forms. New financial models for how to keep a theological school solvent are being created, and new, smaller schools are forming in niche construction, fully adapted to their environments and organically linked to their constituents. Most important, a profound demographic shift is happening among students interested in and willing to pay money (and take on debt) for a theological education. As I write this, increasing numbers of Africans, African Americans, Latinx, Asians, immigrants of many countries—all those formerly designated as minority bodies in white majority spaces—are becoming the majority body in the theological academy. These dramatic shifts cast bright light on the distortion that has always been with us.

No one really saw the distortion as a crisis in theological education, although it was and is a crisis. The crisis that has captured everyone's attention is a different matter and can be summed up with one word: "decline," as in declining enrollment, declining financial resources, declining church and denominational support for seminary education, and declining prestige and cultural recognition for clergy. But the crisis formed by decline is not as crucial as the crisis formed by distortion. In fact, the distortion in significant measure fuels the decline.

The distortion is woven into theological institutions and into our deepest pedagogical impulses.

What exactly is the distortion in formation? It will take time for me to show you this distortion and its strong connection to the crisis of decline in theological education.

It is a distortion that forms between two things.

On one side there is an image of an educated person that propels the curricular, pedagogical, and formational energies of Western education, and especially theological education. That image is of a white self-sufficient man, his self-sufficiency defined by possession, control, and mastery.[1]

On the other side, many people respond to that image by promoting a homogeneity that aims toward a cultural nationalism. This quest for a cultural nationalism or cultural sovereignty inadvertently keeps us captured in the formational energies of white self-sufficient masculinity. Theological education in the West was born in white hegemony and homogeneity, and it continues to baptize homogeneity, making it holy and right and efficient—when it is none of these things. "Hegemony" and "homogeneity" are words that mean control and sameness, a control that aims for sameness and a sameness that imagines control.

Crudely put, theological education vacillates between a pedagogical imagination calibrated to forming white self-sufficient men and a related pedagogical imagination calibrated to forming a Christian racial and cultural homogeneity that yet performs the nationalist vision of that same white self-sufficient man. Theological education, however, is simply living out in microcosm the wider problem that plagues Western education.

From a very particular place in the ecology of Western education, I have spied out the problem at a subterranean level that, like a crack in the earth, runs from one place to another, touching lives and connecting people who live in very different worlds. It is essentially a problem of Western education that runs through theological education. It is a problem, however, that was in fact born of theological education itself.

Ever since Christian missionaries began teaching the faith and translating the Scriptures into the mother tongues of peoples, they formed a dynamic filled with possibilities and problems. As the historians of mission Lamin Sanneh and Andrew Walls pointed out so powerfully, by translating the message of the gospel into the languages of peoples, these missionaries performed a faith that revealed a God who loved peoples in their intimate particularities down to the bone of their words.[2] This Christian God allows the divine life to be spoken in the words of everyone, one people at a time, each translating a revelation into their own tongue—the God of Israel loves you and is also your God. This is the deepest and truest root of theological education: gospel translatability. Translation opens up endless possibilities of boundary-crossing freedom and life.

Translation, however, also opened up endless possibilities of boundary-crossing slavery and death. To be a teacher is to be in a powerful position, and to be also a translator is to be close to ultimate power, the power to call worlds into existence through words, spoken and written. Unfortunately, Christians, especially Christians who would come to be called Europeans, did not handle that power well. In the history of Christianity and its missions, worlds formed around the bodies of teachers and translators. The specific world I am concerned with here is the world of education that formed around the colonial legacies of teachers and translators and gave us Western education and, specifically, theological education.

I want to honor the legacies of women and men who courageously and sacrificially went all over the world and established entire ecologies of education upon which modern educational formations have come to life. But I also want to give witness to the deep horrors they wrought through the educational worlds they formed and the ways we are yet haunted by those horrors. Honor and horror will be strange companions on our journey, as I cast light on the distortion in Western (and theological) education.

Two arguments will be made against what I am arguing in this book. The first is an argument against the accusation against white self-sufficient masculinity. Some will take issue with this characterization, imagining that I am engaging in a form of identity political critique and, by some accounts, a subtle form of hate speech. For these interlocutors, I am lumping together too much, throwing out too many babies with the bathwater, and seeing a problem where a more nuanced appreciation of the complexities of church history, the history of missions, theological and philosophical speculation, and human failings would allow me to appreciate what has been accomplished in Western education generally and, specifically, theological education. Western theological education, these interlocutors will remind us, is the father of Western education, the progenitor of educational institutions, and the foundation of most of the intellectual frames from which forms of critique have grown up. I take this argument very seriously, but I hope to show that it misses many marks; most centrally, it misses the basic point. White self-sufficient masculinity is not first a person or a people;

it is a way of organizing life with ideas and forming a persona that distorts identity and strangles the possibilities of dense life together. In this regard, my use of the term "whiteness" does not refer to people of European descent but to a way of being in the world and seeing the world that forms cognitive and affective structures able to seduce people into its habitation and its meaning making.[3]

The second argument that will be made against this work is that it underestimates the need for cultural autonomy, even cultural sovereignty, in theological education for people discounted by whiteness. Many dear friends will tell me that homogeneity may not be the goal but is still a precondition of self-determination, that peoples of color must stand apart to have the sovereignty that has been denied us in the work of education and so begin formation on the other side of the distortion.

A gospel that is translatable not only shows the beauty of a God who loves and speaks to us in our particularities, it also promises a form of cultural agency for peoples through which they can hear their own voices, know their own thoughts, and see God for themselves, or even see their own gods more clearly. For these interlocutors, I fail to see the need for cultural survival and intellectual respect given the continuing power of white Eurocentric hegemony in the theological academy and the profound failures of Western educational and theological institutions to resist their addiction to assimilating everyone who walks through their doors or clicks on their websites. These conversation partners will argue that I am still promoting a form of hegemony, albeit a more subtle one, that leaves white Western Christianity in the driver's seat. I do not, according to this line of argument, take sufficiently seriously the gods of peoples, their countertheological visions and ways of imagining faith beyond the strictures of theological orthodoxies. For these partners, the effects of the long history of Christian colonialism can only be overcome by a theological educational endeavor that frees peoples from white Christian tutelage. The freedom that these interlocutors seek takes aim at many things and exists on a continuum of liberation from various Eurocentric forms of Christian thought and practice all the way to freedom from Christianity itself. No matter where they are on this continuum, these interlocutors will be impatient with my continuing sojourn in the conceptual spaces and theological places yet inhabited by white European Christianity.

I take very seriously this argument. It illumines the fatigue that plagues sectors of the Western academy where a number of scholars of color carry an abiding skepticism that Christian intellectual formation can be anything other than white European masculinist formation. That skepticism, founded at the opening moments of colonial conquest, yet grows and fosters a quiet despair that moves through the educational ecologies of theological schools. The argument for cultural sovereignty in theological education grows out of collapsing the struggle against whiteness into a struggle for peoplehood. This is understandable, given the ways whiteness has historically destroyed a reality of peoplehood for so many groups. It is the struggle for peoplehood that I seek to address, and in so doing I hope to speak to the fatigue and despair that dog so many scholars of color in the academy. Addressing that fatigue and despair will be a theme running through my argument. I hope to show that the deepest struggle for us all is a struggle for communion.

Theological education is supposed to open up sites where we enter the struggle to rethink our people. We think them again, but now with others who must rethink their people. And in this thinking together we begin to see what we had not seen before: we belong to each other, we belong together. Belonging must become the hermeneutic starting point from which we think the social, the political, the individual, the ecclesial, and most crucial for this work, the educational. Western education (and theological education) as it now exists works against a pedagogy of belonging.[4]

Theological education must capture its central work—to form us in the art of cultivating belonging.

✤

Why did you come here?
I was looking for you.
Who told you to find me?
I am not sure, but I think it was God.

✤

The cultivation of belonging should be the goal of all education—not just any kind of belonging, but a profoundly creaturely belonging that performs the returning of the creature to the creator, and a returning to an intimate and erotic energy that drives life together with God. These words—"intimacy" and "eroticism"—have been so commodified and sexualized that we Christians have turned away from them in fear that they irredeemably signify sexual antinomianism, moral chaos, and sin, or at least the need to police such words and the power they invoke. But intimacy and eroticism speak of our birthright formed in the body of Jesus and the protocols of breaking, sharing, touching, tasting, and seeing the goodness of God. There, at his body, the Spirit joins us in an urgent work, forming a willing spirit in us that is eager to hold and to help, to support and to speak, to touch and to listen, gaining through this work the deepest truth of creaturely belonging: that we are erotic souls. No body that is not a soul, no soul that is not a body, no being without touching, no touching without being. This is not an exclusive Christian truth, but a truth of the creature that Christian life is intended to witness.

I once shared these ideas with some people at a dinner gathering. As I did, one gentleman interrupted me and said, "Intimacy and eroticism is what I share with my wife, not the church." I asked him if he thought holding someone's hand in prayer was an intimate act. No response. I then asked him if listening to someone share their hurts and frustrations, fears and hopes was an intimate act. No response. "Was hearing the words, Sunday

after Sunday—this is my body, this is my blood, take and eat—
was this an erotic act?" He said nothing. Then I asked the most
crucial question at that moment: "To whom do you belong?" To
this he responded, "I belong to myself and to God!"

This theologically trained gentleman needed a better vision
of belonging, a Christian vision.

The belonging I am envisioning here superintends all other
forms of belonging, drawing them to healing light and redeeming life. There is a central image in Scripture that illumines the
trajectory of this creaturely belonging. It is the image that drives
this book. It is the picture of Jesus and the crowd. Take, for example, Mark 5:24b: "And a large crowd followed him and pressed in
on him."[5] Or Luke 5:1:

> Once while Jesus was standing beside the lake of
>   Gennesaret,
> and the crowd was pressing in on him
> to hear the word of God . . .

The crowd is everything. The crowd is us.

*People shouting, screaming, crying, pushing, shoving, calling out to Jesus,
"Jesus, help me," "Jesus, over here." People being forced to press up against
each other to get to Jesus, to hear him, and to get what they need from him.
People who hate each other, who would prefer not to be next to each other.
Pharisees, Sadducees, Zealots, rebels, insurrectionists, terrorists, murder-
ers, tax collectors, sinners all . . . widows, the orphans, the poor, the rich, sex
workers, wonderers, magicians, musicians, thieves, gangsters, centurions,
addicts, magistrates, city leaders, people from all over the Roman Empire—
all pressing to hear Jesus.*

> *Jesus teaches a motley crew,*
> *a vagabond feast of people who*

will be caught together under his word
like holy smoke covering them all,
the smell on their clothes,
on their skin.

Jesus created the condition for the crowd, reflecting God's desire for the gathering. The crowd was not his disciples, but it was the condition for discipleship. It is the ground to which all discipleship will return, always aiming at the crowd that is the gathering of hurting and hungry people who need God. In Jesus and the crowd, we see the creator-creature relationship in its most naked, most powerful form—crying, screaming creature calling to its creator and its creator giving up his own body to his creature. Like a mother offering her body to her hungry child, so the crowd is necessary to see God's overwhelming compassion.

We have failed to see that this is the ground of theological education and of all education that aims at the good. It is the crowd—people who would not under normal circumstances ever want to be near each other, never ever touching flesh to flesh, never ever calling in unison upon the name of Jesus, never ever listening together to anything except Roman edict or centurion shouting command, now listening to the words of Jesus. Yet the crowd is not Christian, nor is the crowd exclusively Jewish. The crowd is not a temporary condition on the way to something else. The crowd is the beginning of a joining that was intended to do deep pedagogical work.

Theological education must be formed to glory in the crowd, think the crowd, be the crowd, and then move as a crowd into a discipleship that is a formation of erotic souls, always enabling and facilitating the gathering, the longing, the reaching and the touching. Our educational settings need to be aimed at forming erotic souls that are being cultivated in an art that joins to the bone and that announces a contrast life aimed at communion. By communion, I mean the deepest sense of God-drenched life attuned to life together, not with people in general but with the people that comprise the place of one's concrete living and the places (the landscapes, the animals, and the built environments) that constitute the actual condition of one's life. Theological education, with its vision of formation properly in its sights, can be an answer to a question Western education has yet to fully comprehend—what is education for?— and can be a response to what Western education has wrought—an educated imagination that is good for some but absent of the many.

Orientation

Let me be the first to welcome you and
ask you
Why did you come here?
Many reasons are available
Take as many as you can carry
Forward

I am here to teach, you are here to learn . . .
I have been searching for
Why did she die so young
in the Lord?

I am here to make sure you understand the differences in
*   Christians*
across the vastness of time, so you can respect that distance
*   . . .*
I want to love and be loved without guilt or fear that God
*   hates me.*

Exegesis, exegesis—I will teach you exegesis, interpreting
texts in contexts . . .

SECRETS

I want to find God so I can kill him
personally thank him for the hell in the—my world.

Pastoral care is a crucial skill I will invite you to ponder
    here . . .
I fought my way off the streets and into this safe space.
This is a safe space, right?

Dogma is not a bad word. I will teach you to think
theologically . . .
I am looking for my body. They took it from me.

The education of Christians is the work of the whole
    church . . .
I hate this, but I am good at it, so I am here.
Take, eat, this is worship . . .
Maybe I can finally get a lover who is a good person.

What makes ethics Christian and what makes Christianity
    ethical,
this is the question for us.
. . . kids older now, my turn to take the unknown road

We are very serious about
connecting you
with communities of faith where . . .
I am schooling until I can find a way out of my debt . . .

You can exercise your gifts.
. . . I have no idea when.

We are a community seeking to build community . . .
I killed people, carved up my soul, so I want to help others
help me

Professor I am thrilled to be taking your class . . .
I am so tired of teaching this,
but I have no way out.

Would you be willing to do a directed study with me?
. . . Every day the classroom calls me,
But so do my bills.

I would like advanced standing, I took this course in
  college . . .
I am waiting to hear if I will have a job next year,
God help me

We are passing out metal straws
Please take one
You will only be able to sip your professors in
Slowly and only little by little
Please force your whole body into the straw
Your professors will be using the same straws
To drink you in small portions.

We theological educators fail to grasp our shared work of cultivating belonging because we are caught up in a series of misapprehensions.

The first thing we misapprehend is the fragment. We who journey in theological education—as teacher, as student, as administrator, or as committed graduate—often fail to realize that we always and only work in the fragments. The first chapter of this book will explore the fragment and why it is so important for theological education. There are three kinds of fragments we must negotiate. The first of them is good and right and the other two have come to us through pain and suffering, yet they are here with us and we must address them as well. There are the fragments of faith, the creaturely pieces of memories and ideas and practices that we work with to attune our senses to the presence of God. Then there are the colonial fragments that have shattered our worlds and which we are constantly trying to unfold and piece together. And then there is the commodity fragment that we struggle against that organizes our processes of exchange and deeply penetrates our visions of relationality. Before and beneath the performing of intellectual traditions or identities, we are fragment workers, working simultaneously with these three kinds of fragments. I argue in this chapter that it is a profound mistake to first imagine ourselves inhabiting theological or even intellectual traditions. Rather, we primarily inhabit fragments. The first fragment is meant to move around us and through us, binding us together in orbits of thinking and acting, remembering and creating. Yet the fragments of faith can help us work with the colonial fragments and help us overcome the effects of the process that constantly creates the commodity fragment. We are fragment workers aiming at patterns of belonging.

The second chapter considers what it means to design educational experiences aimed at cultivating belonging. What do we do with the fragments? Where do they go? They help to form lives through designing new patterns for thinking life together. This chapter reflects on what educational design means in relation to the legacy of colonialism and whiteness, which has led to a second misapprehension—the design of formation.

Theological education has had its formation energies aimed at the art of cultivating "the man who serves." This might sound noble and biblical, but it is far from it. This is pedagogical vision that imagines its work aligned with a gospel direction—Jesus is the one who "came not to be served but to serve, and to give his life a ransom for many" (Mark 10:45)— but the connection between the one and the many, between one who serves and the many served, is imagined and then designed very poorly. This is pedagogical vision caught between an isolating individualism and a sick intellectual performativity. Between these two problems three distorted forms of educational design develop: designs for attention, affection, and resistance.

Together they press us into a soul-killing performativity aimed at the exhibition of mastery, possession, and control with the tacit assumption that this ongoing work of exhibition illumines talent and the capacity for leadership. The problem with forming "men who serve" is not in our diagnostic accuracy for determining leadership capacity or intellectual talent based on their performativity. The problem here is that it cultivates an abiding isolationism at the heart of this view of performativity, which infects everything and everyone in the academic ecology of a school. Everyone is caught up in an exhibition that pushes us always toward isolation.

The design of educational experiences is inextricably bound up with the work of institution building. This work of building institutions is the concern of chapter 3. In recent years much has been written about institutions, especially educational institutions and their importance. But those conversations for the most part have been terribly shortsighted, because they have imagined institutions without reckoning with their deep embeddedness in cultivating white self-sufficient masculinity and binding ideas of efficiency and effectiveness to the performance of that persona. Institutions are caught up in the historical trajectory of a plantation pedagogy that teaches us how to be institutional men, which is how to aim at becoming a master.

The most urgent question about institutions and institutional life within theological education (and indeed all higher education) is not about how we might sustain institutions or restore respect for them. The most urgent questions are about how we should rethink the work of building so that we can move away from the cultivation of an institutional persona that is soul killing and death dealing. How do we form institutional life such that everyone may feel at home in the work of building, sustaining, or supporting an institution without suffering in a tormented gender performance bound up in racial and cultural assimilation? At present, a healthy institutional life not rooted in white masculinist self-sufficiency is a difficult reality to imagine, let alone execute.

Chapter 4 continues the reflection on institutions and the work of building but focuses on the distorted forms of edification, of building in Western educational settings that makes life within our educational ecologies so burdensome. This chapter considers that difficulty of changing the vision of edification that drives Western educational institutions. Faculty, staff, and students form an energy that is like a spiraling wind. This energy, this wind, is a wonderful thing, but unfortunately the motion of that wind has been set in place by the vision and sensibilities of the white master, always turning us in directions that thwart healthy academic ecologies and healthy institutional life. What is needed is a new motion that turns that wind, that institutional energy, toward life together in three crucial ways: (1) how we move into each other's lives, that is, how to think a good assimilation; (2) how we move inwardly and outwardly, that is, how we enact a healthy inwardness; and (3) how we move in new directions, that is, how we enact radical change and the overturning of the prevailing order.

I am aiming at a gathering together of people that is both the *modus operandi* and the *telos* of the formation that should characterize theological education, but before I end this book, I need to consider something else that impedes our realizing such a vision, and that is the convening power of whiteness. Whiteness was formed in the colonial theater with a convening power unprecedented in the world not only in its scale but also in its utter disregard for the convening abilities of other peoples. In the hands of the Europeans, the good of convening joined the bad of imperialism, and from it came a vision of the universal controlled by Europeans. Only they could gather the world, and only they understood the gathering of the world. Europeans not only exploited the differences among peoples but they also created boundary identities between peoples—geographic, physical, cultic, sexual, and theological—that Europeans believed spoke the truth of peoples more accurately than peoples' own accounts of themselves. Religions, races, and nations were created in this operation of whiteness, and we are yet caught in its protocols, protocols that drive forward its imperialist habits of mind. A vision of life together in service to the formation of erotic souls must reckon with the imperialist habits of mind born of whiteness that imagine peoples through boundary identities.

In the final chapter I outline the importance of desire in education, and especially in theological education. It is desire that joins fragments, designs, buildings, and motions together, turning us out toward one another through and in a redeeming Eros. It is desire that could disrupt the imperialist habits of whiteness. Returning to the relation of Jesus to the crowd, I end by pointing out that theological education is a matter of lure and longing deeply embedded in a desire to see God change the lives of those around us, healing the sick, delivering the captives, overturning the powers that be, and raising the dead to new life. That desire to see a changed world must be allowed to find its connection to the desire for one another.

The things I have said here are pithy, compact. My goal will be to unpack them, and in so doing to mark a possible way beyond the distortion in theological education (and Western education), and if possible, to reveal the gift that theological education could be to Western education if we theological educators would ever actually see our important difference and Western education's tragic dilemma. But my task will require that I tell the meaning of the secrets of theological education. I will do so through stories (the beginning of which is indicated by · · ·, the end by · · ·) and poetry (indicated by ❧). I am engaging in a kind of institutional gnosticism, revealing the hidden meaning in the words, actions, counteractions, and conversations that constitute theological academic life. Every story I tell will be both truth and fiction, fiction in the service of truth and truth that demands fiction. I will tell no one's story, but I will tell many stories. No one's truth will be violated or privacy lost, but I will tell the inside and enter the sanctum of hearts, open the closed rooms of desire. I will take pieces from here, slices from there, and weave together as much as is necessary. If you know me and remember our time, please know that any resemblance to actual events is purely coincidental.

Secrets

I have been the keeper of all secrets, secrets that I will take to my grave. I listened to those who needed a safe place to speak their inside, and together we gloried in the inside. All of this I remembered, but I, like so many other scholars, carry a wild memory.

We scholars in the academy have WILD MEMORIES
Ugly-beauty
Unruly things
We remember things SO BIG, and so small
Making us fantastically strange
mutants, we remember
Things that normal creatures could not possibly remember
Things that normal creatures would not possibly want to remember
Things like axioms, theorems, slights, insults
Complex formulations of ideas, compliments twenty years old
The words that made us cry and the words we spoke that made others cry

We engage in conceptual fights with ghosts we never met
sustained over centuries.
We engage in fights with
colleagues now ghosts,
sustained over decades.
We remember sentences
Verbatim,
the hidden,
trying not be found in obscure texts
and the most minuscule acknowledgments
Scholars we loved and hatred for things
so feathery that it takes enormous
concentration to keep them from
floating away.
Our memories are so tightly woven to our feelings that we don't know
where the one begins and the other ends . . .

*We forget sometimes what normal creatures would not possibly forget—
dates of birth and love,
times of kisses and hugs,
this friend moment of gold,
that family time of silver or diamond.*

*Oddly, many of us scholars worry about how other scholars will
remember us.
We forget that all memory depends on the untamed.*

The things I tell are precise accounts while being exact fabrications. All this is rendered with my wild memory. But everything I tell you, *everything*, is the truth. It is truth in the service of moving us to a new place of gathering where our learning is submerged in desiring and desiring becomes what God intends it to be—our eager new home.

1

Fragments

It all begins with him.

. . .

We were coming to the end of a search for a would-be faculty person for a junior position (that is, a position for someone just beginning their teaching career). The selection process came down to two candidates, both wonderfully qualified and talented: an African American woman and an Anglo-American man. Like so many educational institutions at this time in history, especially theological institutions, we were

committed to having a diverse faculty. (Beautiful words.)

So with at least one of these candidates, we had a possibility of enhancing the diversity of the faculty. As part of the selection process, a governing body of the faculty interviewed the candidates. As soon as the interview process was over for both candidates, I knew that the Anglo-American male candidate was getting this job.

❧

I love to tell the story,
Of unseen things above,

CHAPTER 1

Of the words that cannot be spoken,
Of locating the real but unmentionable loves[1]

❧

On the day of his interview, I saw something coalesce in front of me that I had only seen in delicate vignettes until then. What did I see? The young scholar who got that job was a brilliant scholar, but what he performed in his interview was something else.

His was a beautiful presence that played off his appearance, his comportment, and his way of speaking. A tall, dark-haired, baritone-voiced, perfectly groomed bearded man dressed like a professor in the middle of a celebrated career, he spoke with confidence and polished ease. His answers to the questions posed to him exhibited nothing new or particularly insightful, but he answered every question to the letter, as though he knew what would be asked, and his answers exhibited, if not years of reflection, then certainly precise thinking. To think of him as a stereotype would be to completely miss where I am going here, because in point of fact he was not the point.

The point was my colleagues in the room doing the interviewing. They were all white men with the exception of me, another African American man, and one British woman. What I saw in their faces and what I heard in their voices and later in their assessment of him as a candidate was a stunning revelation of a singular truth.

They looked at him longingly and lovingly, admiring his poise, his confidence, seeing in him what they longed to be, and seeing what they thought we the faculty thought the goal of our shared project of formation ought to be. This is not my projection onto their projections. This is what was said as they assessed the candidates.

He captured love in two intertwining ways: by what he said and by the way he embodied his words.

He inhabited a field that studied ancient texts, texts deeply woven into Christians' life of faith. The field he inhabited, however, was and is at war. It is a western front with deep trenches

24

that span centuries and continents and that trap many institutions of higher learning between two warring sides.

On the one side were scholars deeply committed to the scientific study of ancient religious texts (scriptures)—their history, composition, transmission, translation, and interpretation. These scholars carried forward a struggle and a hard-won battle to wrest control of religious and sacred texts from the arbitrary—from people who used words designated as God's word to execute their will to power, their desire for possession, and to gain mind-bending obedience from religious subjects. But like a reform movement turned cult, these scholars banished all who understood theological interpretations *as inherent to* the scientific study of these ancient texts.

On the other side were scholars deeply committed to the theological interpretation of texts, their histories of use by people of faith and their living dance with Christian doctrine. These scholars carried forward the struggle and a hard-won battle to enliven the preaching and teaching of Scripture in churches. They understood that there is no science of the text without holy performance of it in the lives of God-lovers, most centrally Christians. So for these scholars, any who refuse this faith-work, any who deny the responsibility to aid people into a healthy church-centered interpretation of the faith through their Scriptures, are simply obstacles to be overcome. The scholars who inhabit these trenches, however, move in close proximity to exactly the kinds of people that their friends-enemies in those other trenches find to be the problem: scriptural ideologues.

The lines of his disciplinary field were drawn in difficult places for this candidate, but he transgressed those lines beautifully. Here was a young man who showed that he knew the ancient texts (canonical, noncanonical, and ancillary) and how to engage in their scientific study, but who also showed a deep understanding and commitment to the Scriptures of the church that were for the church. He showed wonderful theological sensitivities and sensibilities—very rare for a modern-day textualist. This was the official reason he got the job, which is true.

But this was not the deepest reason he got the job. You see, the African American woman also showed great skill in the scientific study of texts, and also had deep theological sensitivities and sensibilities. She transgressed those same lines, but she transgressed more. (I will return to her later.)

The white male candidate showed more than the black female candidate—more ability and more nuance. This was the official conclusion. But this was not actually the "more" he showed.

At one point in the interview, a colleague asked this candidate about his year and a half studying in a German university. The meaning of another secret was about to be revealed. "What did you learn?" the candidate was asked. This was a rhetorical question. The young man who went to Germany was already an accomplished student. He had already learned his craft. But in Germany he learned his form.

"My seminars in Germany were 'no holds barred,' vigorous debates about the highest technicalities and most important ideas of my field," he said. (*"No holds barred" is an interesting phrase. It describes a match in which wrestlers fight each other using any and every "hold," even those that could kill, paralyze, or maim their opponent.*) "I really saw what rigorous thinking looks like. It was wonderful." My colleagues burst out in approving laughter, except for me and the other African American man. We knew what this meant.

His formation was complete. He had put together some of the fragments out of which the scholarly form would appear—knowledge of various texts, 1.5 years of study in Germany, knowledge of German language, theology, biblical languages, seminars, blue suit, brown wingtip shoes, slow speech, legs crossed, quiet confident comportment. This US-born and -raised scholar even spoke in the interview and during his public lecture with a slight German accent.

❧

He showed himself to be a knower
aiming at mastery,
a mind striving for possession,

and a body in control.
He showed himself to be a brilliant performer of white self-sufficient
masculinity.

The black woman was told thanks but no thanks. Like the guy, she showed something more in her interview, but something not wanted. She wanted to talk about *herself* as integral to her work as a textualist, specifically about the racial condition of the West and how ancient texts and modern interpretations play in and against that condition. Right in front of our eyes at that interview she was making her life a bridge, a safe way across the battle lines of her field and into a new land that included the concerns of those warring sides. She too was putting together the fragments out of which the scholarly form would appear, knowledge of various texts, knowledge of German and French, biblical languages, knowledge of theology, and seminars.

They both were working with fragments,
but her fragment work flowed around her body
illuminating her field and who she was as a scholar working in it.
His fragment work coalesced around his body
concealing him inside white self-sufficient masculinist form
through which he was imagined as
one with his field,
homoousios,
of the same substance as his discipline.

Report Summary: The committee, after careful deliberations and vigorous, honest debate, could see the body of candidate B (for black woman)—but not as a bridge to anything important. But it did see the body of candidate A (the self-sufficient young man) as exactly the body it wanted to be and wanted every student in the school to resemble, intellectually speaking. *How else are we speaking?*

. · .

❧

I felt the anger, the old anger that had been with me from the beginning. What beginning? I don't know when it started. It has always seemed to have been with me, formed at the site of my blackness. And I felt the struggle, the old struggle to keep the anger from touching hatred. My faith—no, Jesus himself—was the wall that kept the anger safe from hatred. Anger yes, hatred no, because if anger touched hatred, I would be poisoned by death himself and become trapped in an addiction that few have been able to escape.

❧

In truth, I too loved this young male candidate at the moment of his performance. I loved him in the precise sense that Pecola loved whiteness in Toni Morrison's novel *The Bluest Eye*.[2] I loved his finish, and I longed to be finished as well—polished like a new car with a powerful engine, one that would be carefully caressed and collectible. I loved how he could gather the love of my colleagues through his performance, and I wanted to gather that same love in a performance like his. There with my colleagues I was caught up in the purest form of intellectual eroticism I had ever experienced. But this was a tragic eroticism. I loved German, loved reading German philosophers and theologians, and loved the sound of the language, though I was never good at it. Like many of my American colleagues, I always looked *longingly* at anyone who had mastered German and Germany, becoming one with the intellectuals there, conversant with their moods and intellectual senses.

There was a sickness present at the moment of that interview. For this was profoundly distorted love. Distorted not in love for

German or German thinkers, but something bound up inside that love. I had learned to love an intellectual form that performed white masculinist self-sufficiency, a way of being in the world that aspires to exhibit possession, mastery, and control of knowledge first, and of one's self second, and if possible of one's world. This was a performance and a destiny in plain sight.

A German university showed my now new colleague the way.

Germany wanted to be a colonial power. For a long time it watched as Britain and France expanded their Lebensraum, their living spaces and their lifeworlds, to the far corners of the world, claiming lands and peoples as their possessions. What also emerged from Britain's and France's colonial holdings was knowledge. This was a strange sort of knowledge, rooted in people and things, stolen, broken into little pieces, mangled, displaced from space and time, and made silent while experts explained to the world what these colonial objects were and what they meant for the world. This was knowledge (fragments) that could build global authority, form worlds, and give imperial voice. Germany wanted voice too. So it sought early to master the fragments.[3]

It has taken me a long time to name this problem because it hides itself so well inside of Christianity, having had a life prior to the emergence of the faith. It grew beautifully and powerfully inside of colonialism and colonial Christianity, took hold inside the educational foundations of the modern West, and now constantly flashes across the cognitive landscape of the educated imagination. The formation of the self-sufficient man has always been the greatest temptation for Christian formation because Christian formation has always been so close to it. It smells like us, sounds like us, draws on our own erotic urges, and moves in the world like we Christians often want to move in the world. It models what we want but not who we are. This chapter aims to begin moving our educational imagination away from that self-sufficient man by focusing on the fragments—the things that constitute the ground of educational work.

Edward Schillebeeckx, the Belgian Roman Catholic theologian (1914–2009), in a little-known essay entitled "Secular Criticism of Christian Obedience and the Christian Reaction to That Criticism," inadvertently outlined briefly but powerfully the dilemma of Christianity's relation to the legacy of the self-sufficient man.[4] He noted that Christianity formed in the shadow of a Hellenistic and, later, Roman vision of humanity's inherent grandeur, with which it would be at odds from its beginnings until now. That vision of humanity's grandeur presented human nobility, its greatness of soul, and its magnanimity to be seen precisely in its self-sufficiency. The self-sufficient man was one who was self-directed, not given to extremes of desire or anger. Focused and clear, he would be independent of others, especially in times in which singularity of purpose, moral vision, or goal demanded one stand against all others. The magnanimous man is centrally characterized by honest assessment of his abilities. He never ever denies his own strength, never pretends to be less than he actually is. He recognizes his own power and uses it wisely.

Schillebeeckx noted that there was already an idea of humility within this frame, and it was not one to be admired. Humility denied human grandeur, undermined the formation of self-sufficiency, and of magnanimous men, and constantly spoke the code of slavery and enslavement. Christianity's troubled task was to show its appeal, given its reputation of being against the formation of self-sufficiency and for promoting what to Greeks and Romans and many others was a repugnant humility. After all, the God of the Christians was a crucified slave who cried and prayed to God for help, not a self-sufficient man. It was a faith that reached toward an obedience that bordered on docility and certainly not the clear singularity and power of magnanimity.

Reconciling the magnanimous man and the Christian man, reconciling inherent human grandeur and godly humility, was a dilemma for Christianity. Schillebeeckx suggested that Thomas Aquinas offered the most compelling option for reconciliation. For Thomas, there is no competition between man's grandeur and the humility he must have in relation to God. Man knows that he has a grandeur, a power, a strength that is his own, that makes his actions genuinely his own, and his creations authentically his by his own hands. But he also knows that in humility all that he has is a gift from God. False humility for Thomas would be to deny these gifts by denying the inherent self-sufficiency of man.[5] This would be sin, but it would also be sin not to live in humility and thanksgiving to God for those same gifts.

To Schillebeeckx, Aquinas had gifted the world with a way to reconcile the Christian faith's and the ancient regime's ways of grasping together the self-sufficient man. Schillebeeckx then noted in this same essay that visions of a self-sufficient man moved forward in European modernity unimpeded by Christianity and carried forward the ancient animosities against the faith. Yet here is where Schillebeeckx did not see what he was actually registering in early European modernity. European Christian settlers to the new worlds of Africa, the Americas, and other soon-to-be-colonized lands, from the fifteenth century forward, were already reconciling the ancient regime and the modern world, already weaving together a pre-Christian and a Christian vision of the self-sufficient man and lodging that weaved vision definitively in its educational visions in the new worlds.

Aspiration is a key engine in intellectual formation.

A vision of the self-sufficient man—one who is self-directed, never apologizing for his strength or ability or knowledge, one who recognizes his own power and uses it wisely, one bound in courage, moral vision, singularity of purpose and not given to extremes of desire or anger—is a compellingly attractive goal for education and moral formation. The power of this vision is that it binds a man to a task, a job, a vocation, or a philosophy that ironically takes the focus off the man, thereby drawing him to a work and a world greater than himself but inextricable from him and his power.

Such formation was absolutely crucial in a (new) world where women and men believed they had been granted by God enormous control over vast areas of land and vast numbers of people, over resources and riches, and been granted the power to kill and enslave countless numbers of people through weapons far more advanced than those wielded by native inhabitants. Such formation was also crucial for reforming native inhabitants away from what this self-sufficient white man perceived as their infantile and hopelessly tribal ways of life that undermined their sense of intellectual independence and individualism.[6]

White self-sufficient masculinity is the quintessential image of an educated person, an image deeply embedded in the collective psyche of Western education and theological education, flexible enough to capture and persuade any and all persons so formed to yield to it. It floats through our curricular imaginations, our pedagogical practice, and the ecologies of our academic institutions. It conceals from us where our true work in education begins—that is, in working in the fragments.

The fragment means many things. There are three kinds of fragments that we work with in the academy. They must never be confused, but neither should they ever be imagined as separate. These fragments together create the lens through which to see our work of formation.

There is the fragment formed by faith itself. This is the first fragment. We have the words of Jesus, the words of the prophets, the stories of Israel, the lives of so many who have called themselves Christian through the centuries—their thoughts in texts, reports and secondhand reports, deliberations, confessions, decisions, meditations, interpretations—*everything is in slices and slivers, pieces and shards.* We have no whole here—no whole picture of ancient Israel, or the prophets, or their families, or Jesus, or his family, or early, middle, or late Christians, or the entirety of their thinking, no full uncovering of their desires, angers, frustrations, hopes, and dreams. No complete picture of any theologian, or heretic, or faithful or unfaithful priest, monk, nun, missionary, mystic. All of it is merely fragments, large and small.

Every teacher knows this. Build a syllabus, year after year, and you will sense this. Teach a class, counsel a student, present a point, resist an idea, applaud an insight, and all of this will be revealed.

. . .

I was invited to consult with a school about curricular matters. The conversation with the faculty turned toward the teaching of church history, and there and then I found myself in the midst of another war. On one side were historians trained in the history of ideas, the development of doctrine, and the relentless analysis of subtle shifts in ideas through the centuries of Christians thinking about their faith. These historians wanted the new curriculum to double down on precisely this kind of historical work—careful consideration of the subtle but crucial shifts in doctrinal thinking that led to the development of orthodoxy and healthy theological thinking. *Build the orthodox mind and thereby build a theologically responsible mind, piece by piece.*

On the other side were historians trained in social history, the history of sexuality and gender, and the history of cultural practices. These historians had no patience with the old ways—with doctrinal developments that ignored the gendered lives, social and cultural contexts, and sociopolitical practices of the ancients. These historians wanted the new curriculum to let in the fresh air of new approaches to thinking ancient Christians in their contexts, allowing us to measure the meanings and constructions of orthodoxy and heterodoxy. *Build the critical mind and thereby build a theologically responsible mind, piece by piece.*

The conversation became heated. Curricular conversations normally do. Both sets of historians wanted to cultivate a theologically responsible mind, but lurking behind those words was the image of the educated man. I was not interested in that image, only the fragments. These dear colleagues lost sight of the profound intellectual work at the heart of theological formation, that of working together in the fragments.

. . .

The point I am pressing toward here is not that all knowledge is fragmentary, partial, and incomplete, and that therefore we need to operate with a chastened agnosticism toward what we know. Nor am I saying that all knowledge is endless fabrication, endless construction, and that our focus should be on the ethics of its creation and deployment. Fragment in this first sense is a reality of being creatures who can only apprehend with our senses—in bites, in touches, in smells, in sounds, and in focused but shifting sight. We live in the reality of these pieces where the world is always too much for us to hold all at once. We creatures live in pieces, and we come to know our redemption in pieces.

> Then he ordered the crowds to sit down on the grass.
> Taking the five loaves and the two fish, he looked up to
>   heaven,
> and blessed and broke the loaves,
> and gave them to the disciples,
> and the disciples gave them to the crowds.
>
> (Matt. 14:19)

God works with these fragments, moving in the spaces between them to form communion with us. The fragments facilitate communion. Too much theological education, however, takes the fragments of faith, aligns them with colonialist aspiration, and invites us to compositions that drain life.

You sought me out, came to my office saying the usual words for a bright student: "I think I would like to do doctoral work." "Why?" I asked. You gave the usual answers. "I like to study." "I like the model of the pastor-scholar." "I would like to be a professor." "I would like to keep my hands in the academy." I felt like Samuel looking at another Saul. So I closed my eyes with my eyes wide open and I listened and smiled. I was waiting for a truth that would join us. I was not waiting for great grades, high test scores, classes with my colleagues here or at your undergraduate institution, scholarly pedigree, language study, international experience, strong recommendations.

FRAGMENTS

I was waiting for this: "I have these questions that refuse to let me go—questions about life and death, urgent questions about the why of a world gone mad and of a faith toying with that madness. I am looking for the place (the discipline) that best houses my questions, the place where I can struggle with them in the intensity of a serious sweat, and then I want to teach in the urgency of those questions." Then I would say to you, "Welcome, my friend, to a truth inexhaustible and a calling clearly identifiable."

There is another fragment formed of colonial power. This is the second fragment. So many people of color understand this fragment. It is life formed in fragment, in memory of loss and in loss of memory where worlds were shattered into pieces: land and animals taken; practice and rituals, dance and songs, ancient word and inherited dream, thoughts and prayers existing only in slice and sliver, piece and shard. *Many of us work in fragments*, trying to tie together, hold together, the witness of our peoples. Weaving the sounds, songs, and stories that are only fleeting echoes of what was. Call it a cultural fragment if you wish. It is serious business—precious saving work—trying to find it, unearth it, and hold it close.

I knew an African ethnomusicologist who told me he could identify and match most of the rhythms of African American music with their originating homes among various peoples on the African continent. The same might be said of dance, or song, or oral, musical, or written phrasing. Then there is the bricolage formed of suffering, the baroque of mixture where displaced and disrobed diasporic cultures bound together their fragments with one another or with the colonial masters and created things to hold things, formed things to say things, wove together things to overcome things.

Slices and shards nonetheless.

Many people come to theological education looking for help with the fragment, hoping that those who teach about their faith can help them reassemble what was shattered, help them gather together what remains. Unfortunately, too many of us who teach and administrate have no idea of this crucial and complex work of reassembling fragments.

The institution I served as academic dean exists not far from at least two different Native American peoples, both of whom had very large and vibrant Christian communities, but at no time during my many years at that institution were we able to attract Native American students in anything but the tiniest of numbers. I had a meeting with a Native American alum and a Native American student about how we might bring in more students from their community. They both gave me a look that carried both sadness and a sense of ridiculousness. "There is no help for us here," the student said in reply to me. The alum not only agreed but added more sober words still: "The work we need to do cannot be done here."

. . .

I remember Maria, raised conservative Baptist in Jamaica, in a Christian world where everything African was seen as primitive, backward, and anti-Christian, but she knew better. She had degrees in cultural anthropology, and she wanted her faith to speak to the beauty and majesty of her African past and African diaspora present. So she found her way to divinity school in hope of help and support in finding a Christian voice that remembered the African. But now she was at my office door telling me she was leaving school. Four semesters done, with only two to go in a master of divinity program, she had had enough. Maria had been told by her professors that (a) she had a naïve monolithic vision of Africa that failed to take seriously its complexities and differences, and that (b) "retrieving an African heritage" was not a matter to be dealt with in a divinity school. "You should return to your own community to do that work," they said to her.

. . .

❧

I felt the anger, the old anger that had been with me from the beginning. What beginning? I don't know when it started. It seemed always to have been with me, formed at the site of my blackness. And I felt the struggle, the old struggle to keep the anger from touching hatred. My faith—no, Jesus himself—was the wall that kept the anger safe from hatred. Anger yes, hatred no, because if anger touched hatred, I would be poisoned by death himself and become trapped in an addiction that few have been able to escape.

My colleagues did not understand what Maria was asking. She carried no romanticism about Africa or Africans, and she thought that this divinity school community of Christians was her community. She wanted the fragments of faith to be joined to the other fragments, the remaining pieces of her peoples. She wanted faculty and students to join her and guide her in reclaiming and retrieving what had been broken into pieces and scattered to the wind—the sounds, sensibilities, wisdom, knowledge, and life strategies of multiple peoples made black by a colonialist brush. But no one understood this as theological work to be done. One colleague even said to me, "Well, she should've gone to an HBCU (historically black college or university) seminary or divinity school. Where they do that kind of work." This colleague understood neither HBCU schools nor our own work.

This fragment work is a deeply Christian calling, born of the tragic history of Christians who came not to learn anything from indigenous peoples but only to instruct them, and to exorcise and eradicate anything and everything that seemed strange and therefore anti-Christian. We Christians created a problem that we are obligated to address. The theological sensibilities of too many peoples made Christian under these destructive conditions continue this destruction by perpetuating fear and disgust for their own people's practices and turning away critical, always critical, of them as they look and listen to those voices most similar and familiar to their own. Not everything can or should be made Christian, but too many peoples never got the chance to do that discerning work before everything was shattered into pieces.

CHAPTER 1

Some have always worked to turn these fragments against the faith in hopes of finding what was lost and securing a vision of a world fortified against the formation of a Christian and freed from its derogatory logics and suspicious gazes. These fragment workers believed against Christianity, not within it.

I have watched many a student become converted to this quest *while in the midst of their theological education*, becoming secret agents for the fragment, looking and hoping for ways to put together *an alternative* to a Christian world or an *alternative* Christian world to the Christian one that they had inherited. This is the perennial struggle at the site of this fragment work.

I sought you out, asked you to come to my office immediately after class, after your presentation. I heard, I saw, I bore witness to a truth: you are called to teach. You were not sure about this, not convinced this was your thing, an outfit in your size. But I know the sound of a teacher, one who speaks a word for the weary. You see, a teacher sees to the heart of the matter and pulls things through to other things and then more things, connecting what others do not even see as connected—suffering to hope to structures to desire to agents to joy, and all to God in the depths, always in the depths. You need to know that this is rare. In my entire career I have only sought out three people, four at most, to say what I am compelled to say to you: teach! Maybe you would have come to your calling without this moment of intervention, but I could not take the chance that you would go another way, away from the students being prepared for you. Others walk the path, but you must run, because the hour is urgent and your voice is needed.

. . .

I remember Harold, a tall and elegant black man, chosen early to inherit his father's ecclesial throne. He was a churchman to his bones, but now, in his final semester, something had been unleashed. He sought an African throne in an African American home for a Christianity that needed to be rebaptized. He gave my colleagues hell. In every course and in every class, he decreed his blackness. He would read only black authors, engage in only Afrocentric conversations, demand that a rationale be given for why yet more white voices were the central bearers of wisdom.

He prophesied to me: My church will rewrite both worship and ritual to capture the beauty of the African. We will meditate on the words of wisdom from the diaspora. We will articulate a faith that speaks redemption to the black body.

I appreciated everything Harold wanted to do, and as I listened I longed for a school that would have invited this fragment work from the beginning, but to a different end.

. ˙ .

Harold wanted what Maria wanted what my Native American student wanted what my Korean student wanted what my Ghanaian student was fighting for what my student from Peru wanted what my Maori student believed she was achieving what my South African (Khoisan) student wanted—to join the cultural fragments to the fragments of their faith in new and life-giving ways. Yet I wanted for them all a greater hope than only restoring a sense of indigenous worlds now in pieces. I wanted a drawing of those pieces together, a throwing of them into the air, an allowing of the Spirit of the living God to take those pieces and fit them together in new and life-giving ways that would be familiar, singing familiar songs, remembering peoples and lands, struggles and hopes, but also new, with new songs, new futures that would mark a path toward what Christianity could be at the site of fragments. The work of joining fragments aligned with the work of loving and learning together: this was the fragment work I wanted to see.

This is not the only sense of this second fragment. It is not only life formed in fragment but also life formed as fragment, that is, life formed in reduction. The colonial operation that shattered indigenous worlds into object, artifact, and archive also by that same operation reduced people to racial objects, the fragment *sine qua non.*

Racial Fragment: Worlds have been enfolded like pieces of paper into smaller and smaller blocks, and peoples have been collapsed onto a racial body not made with their own hands. Hundreds and thousands of different peoples have been collapsed into blackness, or whiteness, or something in between those "nesses." Identities have been formed fit for a new work and a new way of being: for possession, commodification, and evaluation. What does it mean to have one's body reduced to a racial body, reduced to a fragment? We work against this fragment, having been forced to live as it and in it. Whiteness is fragment life, too, but it hides it well. Racial existence is fragment life, and these fragments are easily weaponized and mobilized to destroy life and conceal options for living.

. . .

I need to return to Harold, for this black man who would be Afrochurch king also made life difficult for his student colleagues. Harold administered racial tests to everyone. He tested how other black students would preach, talk, walk, sing, pray, dress, and play. He commented on what food they would and would not eat, what music they listened to, what hymns and gospel songs they knew and did not know, what preachers, teachers, evangelists, prophets, bishops, singers, groups they had learned about and from, and most devastatingly, he judged who was fit to carry forward the legacies of blackness, of African-ness, of diaspora hope.

Nobody paid attention to Harold on the surface of things, but everyone did in the quiet of the doubts that always permeate seminary or divinity school life. I wanted Harold to live a different kind of fragment life, one that would resist the reduction, war against the test, and allow himself to be unfolded, opened out to a blackness that cannot collapse but that flows like water into everything and everyone without fear and fear's unruly child, the need to control.

. . .

There is a third fragment born of the work of reduction. This is the commodity fragment. This is the fragment formed by the colonialists who came to the new worlds and in an act of creation as powerful as God's turned the whole world into commodities—not actual commodities but commodities in potential—a whole world that could be possessed, because everything could be stolen. And much of it was stolen. This fragmentation gave birth to a new focus—to see the planet as both knowable and saleable at the same time. The history of modern colonialism made knowing a thing and owning a thing two sides of the same coin, and examining a thing and producing a thing two sides of a related coin. This fragment work has yielded tremendous knowledge of a vast number of *things*, but it has also formed isolating life through isolating ways of looking at life. Western education is education in this fragment, and we who inhabit the world of theological education broker in it as well.

*To know a thing is
to possess a thing
(They took our land, our bodies, our stories, our rituals, our tools)
is to sell a thing
(our dance, our music, our sweat, our passion, our hopes, our dreams)
is to have the power
(our birds, our horses, our plant mothers and tree fathers, our loud
streams and quiet rivers)
to discard
a thing
(our blood, our cells, our brains, our skulls, our teeth, our shit)
and then find
a thing
(our anger, our courage, our creative resistance, our allegiance, our
loyalty)
and resell
that thing or*

(our sight, our sound, our fear, our faith)
give that thing
away or have that
thing stolen
(it was stolen from the beginning)
that was not a thing to begin with
but was
my life.

Education is always education in commodities. This is now inescapable. The lives of peoples have been shattered into pieces and have been shaped for intellectual exchange. We must work against its deepest effects, to turn us into intellectual merchants untouched by the fragments we touch. We teachers can easily become fragment workers who deepen in students the possessive logic that governs Western life: *to know a thing is to possess a thing.*

. . .

I remember Della and Ana Paula. Della was a white woman and Ana Paula a Latina. Della found her way to divinity school after a few years of working in a pharmaceutical lab. She had big dreams but a very quiet voice, almost imperceptible. Her years in school learning biology and botany and her time in the lab had not exposed her to the fine joy of extended writing or even reading for that matter. Ana Paula's journey was different. Born in Mexico, she had worked in the corporate accounting world in banking for a few years, but now sensed a call to ministry, and was terribly unsure of herself in the divinity school space. She moved through the hallways with tentative feet as though each step touched broken glass. Della and Ana Paula were in my office because they had plagiarized from a common source, a student paper passed around in the underground market of the divinity school. There was no need to deny it. They both knew it. But I knew why they used this source, even though using it had unintended consequences.

Plagiarism haunts the academy, and especially the theological academy, as an offense within an offense, a taking within a taking. There has always been an irony to the offense (the crime) of plagiarism within the world of the reductive and commodified fragment. Plagiarism is the act of taking the ideas, words, and voice of another without clear and precise acknowledgment that they are the source. But what does it mean to take the ideas, words, and voice of another in a world and in educational systems that were formed by theft and shaped by a taking that continues to this very moment? Schools in so many parts of the world exist on stolen lands, taken from indigenous peoples who each day see the land no closer to their hands. Plants and animals, objects and archives exist in the storage facilities of schools, having been obtained without any rituals of request, no promises of care and return, and no consequences to turning them into waste once they prove useless. Every day, peoples of the black diaspora hear and see their ideas, images, creativity, gestures, stories, styles, moods, music—its phrasing, its rhythms, its chord changes— their dance, their fighting and loving stances copied and copied again, turned into money, but not in their hands. But no one who does this is brought to an academic dean for adjudication. I got the secondary stuff, the theft inside the theft.

So I said to Della and Ana Paula, "The goal of these exercises in writing is to help you find your own voice as you interact with the voices of the writers you are reading." They had not located their own voices. Both were looking for words to hide their words, looking for a voice on the page to make their voice acceptable.

. . .

We *should* take plagiarism seriously, not first because it is theft, but because it is a painful absence of voice alongside other voices. But finding and strengthening voices involve more than learning how to negotiate commodity fragments that present ideas first as possession, words first as property, and voice as that which you can only gain once you own the words and ideas. The work of formation begins with linking together fragments of faith to cultural fragments and both to hopes of resisting the reductive fragmentation of life codified through our educational processes, a fragmentation that aims at reproducing the singular truth of the commodity fragment: to know a thing is to possess a thing.

If we teach fragments and teach against fragments, what does that mean for those who imagine themselves teaching within traditions?

It is a pedagogical and theological mistake to imagine tradition prior to the fragment.

We who teach and learn in theological education settings, should we envision ourselves as teaching in and toward a tradition, whether Catholic, Eastern Orthodox, Protestant (Presbyterian, Methodist, Baptist, Pentecostal, etc.), or liberal or conservative? This question has been with us for a few decades now, ever since the emergence of Alasdair MacIntyre's moral philosophy and its travels deep into theological and religious studies.[7] Unfortunately, the use of tradition in theological education has most often been to promote white self-sufficient masculinity in search of a coherence that would make us safe from seeing our fragment work and conceal what the fragment aims toward: communion, the working and weaving together of fragments in the forming of life together.

· · ·

I remember Mark and Bobby. Mark was from Indiana, raised on a farm, a beautiful thing, and Bobby was from DC, raised in a sequestered and very white suburb. They were both wonderful guys. Each young white man was serious about his Christianity and serious about (as they both told me) "racial reconciliation." I really liked these young men, each aiming his life at ministry. Mark was raised Methodist and Bobby Southern Baptist, but both were tired of tired Christianity, one that lacked clear commitment to the traditions of the church, robust theological thinking, and a form of ministry that actually formed seriously reflective Christians. So they sought a tradition that made sense, because their churches of origin no longer held hope for them.

I watched as they tried on several. Like guys trying on jeans at an Old Navy store, they explored several denominations present on the divinity school menu. Mark finally settled on Episcopalian and Bobby on Eastern Orthodox. They both came to me to rework their programs to fit their new formation in collaboration with their new denominational requirements. In their final semester, I again had them in a course. But now they were different.

Bobby constantly quoted early church writers like they were Scripture and spoke of the demise of the theological foundations of Western civilization due to liberalism. Mark agreed mostly with Bobby but saw the church "in the West" as ineffective because it lacked a robust liturgical awareness that could permeate daily life. They both still wanted to engage in the work of "racial reconciliation," but now they understood that the liberalism infecting the church had to be dealt with before any substantial reconciliation work could be done.

I was glad they had found new ecclesial and theological homes that seem more hospitable to their hopes. But they had also found something else. They were now traditioned men. Now they looked at many of their student colleagues as nice people who lacked a clear sense of being in a tradition. Now they also listened to their divinity school colleagues differently, through a filter: Did their colleagues speak from within an ecclesial tradition or from within the broader Christian tradition, or did they speak from within the chaos of liberalism and its damaging lack of tradition? Did they understand who they were as bearers of a tradition or were they afloat in a sea of emotivism and fragmented ideas?[8]

. . .

These wonderful guys could no longer see themselves in a shared project of life with the other students. Their vision of communion was now denominationally bound and executed through a constrained intellectual vision that turned everyone into possessors of a tradition, aiming at its mastery, and looking for some signatures of control in a chaotic world. Yes, Mark and Bobby were happier now. They had found rest in a place greater than themselves that delivered on a promise of coherence in life and thought that they imagined was the purpose of their formation in theological education. They each believed (as they said to me) that "ministry was not about them but about being the witness to a tradition, a higher calling than the individual, and bound to live a life turned toward a long obedience."

They had become him.

It could be that forming people in ecclesial traditions and the Christian tradition more broadly is the best way to imagine theological education, but until we wrestle with the man lurking inside a tradition, performing himself in the quest for a maturity that has been presented to theological education and all Western education as the goal of its formation, we will lock students in a formation that will take much more than it will give and that will deny us all the gift of working with the fragments. As we turn to our next chapter, I want to press more deeply into a formation work that begins to turn away from this self-sufficient white man and sees the swirling fragments. This new formation aims at designs that work with the fragments, turning them all toward an elusive goal—life in a place of communion.

2

Designs

I was inside it.

. . .

It happened at the beginning of one semester, well into my years as an academic dean. I was in my office early one morning, praying at my desk, in hope, fear, and excitement at the start of student orientation for the new academic year. Today would be my turn to introduce the curriculum, the faculty, the degree programs, and the strategies for learning here, my turn to speak of the beating heart of theological education. Six thirty a.m.—praying quietly, carefully, and then a knock at my door, not the main door that opens from my assistant's office but the private door from the hallway that leads directly into my office. I ignored the knock—must be wrong door, I thought—but it came again with authority and consistency. I got to the door quickly, opened it, and there stood a man I had never seen before, but I knew exactly who he was. I had felt his presence before.

He smiled, stepped into my office, walking past me. He sat at my desk. White flowing hair, perfectly manicured full white beard—he wore a gray suit with bright silver buttons, thick silver belt, beautiful ruby blood-red cuff links on his sleeves. He leaned back in my chair. "Tell me about that dream, Willie," he said, speaking with the full sound of a southern gentleman, each word carrying a plantation cadence.

"As I prayed, I saw the hand of God reaching down from heaven toward the divinity school," I said. "Go on," he replied. "Then I saw another hand emerge from this building where we are right now. That hand grabbed the hand of God by the index finger. I then saw that hand bend back God's finger until it broke. Then I woke up." The man then started laughing, a knowing laugh. He looked me straight in the eyes and said, "This is my school."

I opened my eyes, startled by a knock at the door. "Your 8:15 a.m. appointment is here. Do I need to make any other copies for today's presentation for you?" she asked. I said no. Every year at the end of my presentation during orientation week for new students, I would give the same speech, which ended with the following words:

> The people who inhabit this educational institution come from all over the world, and they make this place home. Friends, this is now your home. Listen to me! You belong here! This is now your home. If anyone here does anything to make you feel like you do not belong here and that this is not your home, please tell me!

I said this for me just as much as I said it for them, especially after that visit.

· · ·

I bore witness to it—the energy of a design that conjured a presence.

As an academic dean, I was able to negotiate that design from a different plateau, war against it with different weapons. But before the deanship, it was hand-to-hand combat. Every year I sadly said good-bye to the graduating seniors. I would miss many of them, not primarily because I had grown close to them, but because I had convinced the good ones to respect me, hear my words, trust my judgments, and thereby lessen the burden of my teaching. But each fall, I would have to start over again, convincing—going to intimate war with many new students. The war with them would kick up the war within me, over legitimacy, certainty, and clarity. This second-layer war is part of the hidden tax of teaching while black, as Nancy Lynne Westfield notes in her groundbreaking edited text, *Being Black, Teaching Black*.[1] But it is more than a hidden tax; it is the struggle with the longitudinal effects of colonial design. Modern theological education has always been inside the energy of colonial design. Colonial design is not one thing but many things organized around attention, affection, and resistance, each aiming, each navigating—each a design that designs.[2]

These are not bad words—"attention," "affection," and "resistance." Indeed, they are energies that should drive educational design. Unfortunately, these energies have been drawn into a distorting creativity that slowly drains us of life by pressing us to perform a particular kind of man. Turning away from that man and toward a creativity that opens toward more life is where the work of design begins. The goal of this chapter is to consider that turning, beginning with attention.

. . .

I remember Thelma. She was not at my institution but asked me to help her, mentor her as she began her first year of teaching. I wanted to help her, a white Baptist woman, newly minted PhD in hand, soon to begin teaching theology at a small Baptist college and seminary. Her courses for both undergraduates and seminarians were filled with men. Her school still found women in theological leadership a hermeneutic challenge and an existential crisis. But the school wanted to do better, so they hired Thelma and put her in the classroom to do better for the students.

The students challenged her every breath.

Her first day they questioned every aspect of her syllabus and every point in her opening lecture. She "stiffened her spine" and soldiered through the first day, then promptly went to the bathroom and threw up. She went back to her office, sat in her comfort chair, and called me, crying. I encouraged her, told jokes to lighten the moment, reminded her that she was not alone. There was a senior woman on faculty at her school (the only other woman in the seminary), Metela, who was in Christian formation and who had been at that school for twenty-plus years. I urged Thelma to contact Metela immediately for support and help. Dead silence. Then, "She is not a serious scholar," Thelma said. I knew Metela and I knew these words—"serious scholar." Thelma with one sentence had spoken the notorious intellectual hierarchy that imagined disciplines like theology high and lifted up above disciplines like Christian education. Thelma had barely met Metela, but she had learned to see through the eyes of that hierarchy and concluded that the woman was not scholarly enough to help her in this struggle.

A few months later, I heard her give a talk at a professional meeting. Her magnificent armor was now fully in place—her every word exact, her use of theological ideas very responsible, and her comportment extremely guarded, beautifully aligned with someone who constantly taught under fire. She was surviving. Rigorous, serious, scholarly—formed yet forming.

.   .   .

Most conversations about design in theological education imagine design at the point of a syllabus, or interactions with students, or evaluative procedures, all of which are important. But there is another design that superintends those other sites of design. It was this superintending design that introduced Thelma to a horror that she would soon normalize. It was a design that aims to teach her and us what to see and what to ignore, especially in ourselves.

The haunting presence that met me at my desk: this is his design.

He moves in the intimate spaces between dream and hope, dedication and wonder, surprise and curiosity, never appearing as what he is, a usurpation, an arrogance bound up in seeing something at a glance and then too quickly turning away to summarize what was seen. There is a form of evaluation, born of colonialism, born of whiteness, that permeates Western education, distorting both a mind at work and the perception of a mind at work. The European colonial settlers formed horror in this evaluative form. The horror is that they showed us how to look for and at something called intelligence and intellectual ability, and, in the process, they took something from us, the desire to pay attention, constant full attention to one another.

Doctoral Seminar
time for a Hearing, your Honor
Nervous Energy
quivering
until the room
levitates downward with
doctoral students lost in running
a tight circle, underground, faster and faster
I will ask a question—
"Will I sound intelligent, like I
belong to the room, filled with
bitten apples, all staring at me
with bright light?" I sweat
waiting for my slender opening
to give the sound of thought and
prove something to no one
in particular. Until the day
comes when I stop
listening to fears and listen to voices
including my own.
Some never hear the sound of
Intelligence

To become a scholar or a teacher or a student means that you desire to pay attention and to yield your very life to the complete work of paying attention. It is a glorious journey, being guided and hopefully someday guiding others into the art and romance of paying attention to the little and the big, the tiny and the overwhelming of the world. It is the road less traveled, but a road not crooked but straight for all those who will hear not with ears, and see not with eyes, but with desire.

European colonial settlers raped attention, forced it into an embrace it did not want. I don't use this brutal language lightly, because "rape" is too dense a word and a reality ever to use flippantly. But only such a word captures the horror pressed on intellectual life in the moment of colonialist enclosure where peoples were determined to be stuck or in stages of development, predisposed to excellence or mediocrity and forced to believe that old world Europe and its new world allies held the truth and transcendence of the human and the world itself. But this tragedy meets us in the now, precisely in an assimilation that defines serious, rigorous, scholarly—not with a broad beautiful vision of paying attention, but through a strangled, suffocating vision that defines these ideas by a relentless Eurocentrism.

· · ·

I finished my years as an academic dean, and after a time of rest and recovery I came back onto the faculty. At the end of the fall semester of my return, the graduate faculty was having its yearly meeting. The purpose of the meeting was to discuss the doctoral program, curricular matters, our relation to the broader university graduate school, and recruitment of students and faculty. One colleague raised concern over how students were meeting the language requirements, passing German and French (which under particular circumstances may be replaced with Spanish). He was very worried that with the advent of electronic dictionaries students would be able to "cheat the tests." His exact words were, "Our students need to know the scholarly languages." I looked at my close friend on the faculty, another African American man, and we shared a smile and then a quiet laugh at these comments. But then things got serious. Each person who responded to this colleague's concern used the same phrase, "the scholarly languages." A dear colleague who taught Buddhist studies leaned over to me and whispered in my ear, "What the hell do they mean by the scholarly languages?"

The conversation then turned ridiculous. One colleague suggested that we ban the use of electronic dictionaries; another wanted to limit students to only one dictionary, to be determined beforehand by the faculty; and then finally the faculty person who started this concern threw down the ultimate gauntlet. "I think they should take the test without any dictionary or any translation aid. Either they know the language or they don't." Silence. I had come back from sabbatical, but I was tired again.

There was a secret the meaning of which was hidden in this conversation. It was another war that yet rages in sectors of the theological and religious academy. It is a war between theological and religious studies. The war looks different in different places, but where I was dean the war was over theological incursion and conquest. Some religious studies faculty colleagues feared that the divinity school was taking over the shared work and ownership of doctoral education and filling the ranks of doctoral students with Bible-believing, orthodoxy-loving, evangelical-leaning eager young scholars who, because they were all that, were incapable of serious, rigorous, and scholarly work. Such work, they believed, requires an objectivity and therefore an imagined freedom from normative, or confessional, or traditioned thinking. As one religious studies colleague was fond of saying, "If you believe the stuff, you can't study the stuff." Of course, for some colleagues this included all religions—all must be purified of believers in the academy.

So the argument over languages concealed a hope that if we make language study as "rigorous" as possible, we can weed out the believers and force the divinity school back into the confessional shadows and out of the pure light of the scientific study of religion. The flaw here (among many) is that divinity faculty were just as committed to the "scholarly languages" as their religious studies colleagues, so this was a contest aimed at absurdity from the beginning. But it was a deadly absurdity.

What broke open the contest and revealed the absurdity that we could all see from the beginning was the comment of one colleague, who gently noted that she had a doctoral student studying early twentieth-century Mormonism and wasn't sure how the "scholarly languages" would help her work. More silence. But she quickly added that she was all for learning these languages. Then she smiled.

. . .

Learning languages can help one learn to pay attention, as Simone Weil so eloquently noted about learning anything from Latin to Greek to geometry.[3] But the discussion of language study I witnessed was not about the beauty of attention, but about the colonialist horror of it.

. . .

I remember Mr. Yoo. He came to my office near the beginning of the semester. A Korean man in his early forties, Mr. Yoo urgently needed to see me to make a request. He needed, he said, an English tutor to help him with his speaking and especially his writing. He had found out from other international students that I had quietly (out of my budget) paid for a tutor for some the previous semester. I wondered why he needed it. His words and his voice seemed sure-footed in English. Then Mr. Yoo showed me a paper he had written for a class. The paper showed violence, red-pen words bleeding everywhere, comments strong and in many cases inappropriate. There were some grammatical mistakes and messed-up phrases but nothing to deserve these written comments from the teaching assistant for the class. Then I looked at him. Mr. Yoo was crying, apologizing to me for his poor academic performance, reciting to me the precise words the teaching assistant had said to him about his writing: terrible, juvenile, not at the level of graduate work, ill-prepared to be here. I knew Mr. Yoo. He spoke and wrote in Korean, Chinese (Mandarin and Cantonese), French, Italian, and Swahili, having lived in all the places that these languages call home.

I felt the anger, the old anger that had been with me from the beginning . . .

My first words after his tears and his apologies were "On behalf of this school, its entire faculty, and especially me as the academic dean, I apologize to you and beg for your forgiveness for the way you were treated. No one should ever speak or write to you in this way."

I knew the professor of this class and the teaching assistant as well (at my former institution we called them preceptors, an ancient designation and beautiful sentiment—one who taught the foundations). The professor lived in the frustrating stage of his career in which he struggled to adapt to change. The students in his classes were not formed like he was, did not have insight into the stories, anecdotes, and sensibilities he shared, and presented something that he did not want—the necessity to work more diligently at communicating and designing his classroom for learning. He focused all his frustration on student writing and demanded that his preceptors bring down the full weight of the law on bad writing. The doctoral student was struggling as well. He had failed one of his preliminary examinations and was feeling the slow but sure abandonment of his doctoral director. He knew it was only a matter of time before he would get the email asking him to stop by his director's office and he would be told that it might be better if he found someone else to work with. He was in that delicate place that all doctoral students enter when they feel the abyss of nothing all around them, knowing that they cannot go back but unsure about whether they can or even want to push on to finish the program. I knew this doctoral student, encouraged him to continue, and wanted the best for him. But now?

The professor and the doctoral student turned their frustration toward this student and destroyed what should have been a gift—writing, thinking one's own thoughts with the thoughts of another. This was, however, the design of the man in my chair. Worlds have been won by serious, rigorous, and scholarly thinking, but even more worlds have been lost through the narrowing of what those words mean and look like.

. . .

It only takes one encounter with the man in my chair for a student to lose hope, only one time to be told or shown or treated as though they are not smart enough, mature enough, prepared enough to be in the theological academy. Even if such students remain in school, we have lost them. I have shed many tears over that loss, and seen too many students lose attention and turn their educational journey into a prison sentence—doing their time and looking toward its end. When students fall hard into academic despair, it is because they have had their expectation shattered: schools that claim to pay exquisite attention to the world and to God often fail to see them or journey with them in the life art of attending.

They lose attention because many of their teachers have lost attention, shed it in the heat of a formation that narrowed intellectual excellence down to one kind of performance, one kind of white body-mind. All of us have been told in the face of this formation to toughen up, to become hard-nosed, to desensitize in an environment grasping for the goal of cold hard truth. But this is one of the main reasons why theological education fails and is failing. It forms an unreal world of petrified attention inside the real world, a real world calling us to attend to the wonders of a God working in the place never released from the rain of divine presence.

Hopeful Eye

Child of a Professor
Eye on you
Focused from birth
Seen precise from the beginning
Never uncorrected, never
quite right.
Legacy of thought, night of
reading, day of talking at every meal, any snack.
The academy is not a home, but your skin.
You became what you are,
a voice in teaching space
so much good possible
if only you had new eyes.
But now your eye is brutal-exacting,
crude knife precision
patiently suffering no slow.
You kill, quietly,
destroy without meaning it.
You passed every eye test, except
the one that matters.

Some of you escaped,
killed the Father-Professor
before he came to see through you
(though he lurks in the shadow waiting to possess you).
Your life wages war, never
on your field but against him.

CHAPTER 2

Fight on!
We need you to win, today
And tomorrow?
We will see

❧

. . .

I was talking to a law professor, a well-published, highly respected colleague who explained to me the way he designs his
classes and especially the kind of intellectual exchange he wants
in the study of law. He believed it would also be applicable for
divinity. He knew I had been an academic dean and had been in
the academy for over thirty years, but he felt the need to share
this with me, and he used the example of a black woman student
to do it. "There was this black woman in my seminar. Let's call
her Sylvia," he said, "and I came at Sylvia just as I did every other
student in this class, questioning her presumptions, challenging
her ideas, objecting to her conclusions. I was unrelenting. In one
very heated exchange with me in the class, she burst into tears.
Some people froze, others looked visibly upset" (either because
she cried or that he had made her cry, I was not sure from his
story). "But Sylvia spoke to me out of her tears in front of the
other students and said, thank you for being the first professor
here to at least take me seriously." His chest swelled with pride
and satisfaction as he told me this story. His conclusion: "Today,
political correctness and identity politics are destroying the possibility of real intellectual formation. Students must be taught to
see what is actually important."

. . .

The tragedy here was not found in his style of debate, with its
vigorous and heated exchange of ideas, or even his pedagogical commitment to a modified medieval *disputatio*, which is in

fact a beautiful discursive practice, a useful method for organizing ideas, and an able guide into certain kinds of conceptual
frames.[4] The tragedy is the narrowing of intellectual formation
to a form of attention cultivated through brutality, through a
design that demands Euro-masculinist gesture as the required
carrier of this student's ideas, her creativity, and her search for
understanding.

We should work toward a design that aims at an attention that
forms deeper habits of attending to one another and to the world
around us. For some what I am pressing toward here makes the
simple overly complex and leans toward being obsessively ac-
commodating to students and a wider society already formed in
and poised toward more forms of entitlement. Sometimes people have to be forced to reckon with their shortcomings, their
failing, and their ignorance and be invited to work harder than
ever to achieve excellence of mind and body. I understand the
sentiment in this perspective. Paying attention requires everything. For scholars who have given their life to study, we know
the respect that is required to inhabit a discipline deeply. We who
teach always live close to the temptation to lose patience with
those who do not see or sense the urgency of intellectual work or
who play in disrespect at the sites of our sacrifice. But our paying
attention also requires a commitment to be patient in weaving
deep lines of connection between what we teach, whom we teach,
and the world we inhabit together with them. It is the promise
we make to the world and to God when we say to ourselves that
we want to know and we want to understand. Even with such a
commitment, our knowing is always as creatures, fragile creatures. We always understand in fragility. Which requires that we
hold each other up in our striving to know, to understand, and
to pay attention.

. . .

I remember Frank. He came to see me one hour before his sched-
uled class. He had been at the school for decades, taught a legion

of students and was deeply beloved, and for good reason. He was an excellent teacher—patient, careful, attentive, gracious, and relentless in making sure students stuck with the work, and it was difficult work. Frank taught languages, Mesopotamian and other ancient languages that only a few people in the world could teach. Over forty years of working in the rare and handling the raw—manuscripts, slices of phrases, and word pieces within pieces within pieces that defied deciphering, unless you were a high priest or priestess of the unseen—helped Frank see meaning in little marks that gestured toward a single letter. Frank amazed me. But now I wondered at Frank in a new way. Why was he here?

After good solid southern pleasantries, we got down to business. Did he need something, a preceptor (teaching assistant) perhaps? "No, my class is small as usual. Five students, brave souls all." Silence, as I waited to know. Frank put his head down, capturing my carpet with his gaze. "Willie, I can't remember. I can't remember anymore." I knew what this meant. The world he knew so well required a memory. The lifeblood of a scholar is her memory. Through it flows the issues of life. *Wild memory is our power.* For Frank, his memory contained the hidden treasures of how to decipher the undecipherable, and meanings and phrases and false words and real words, and paths of translation to take and not to take, none of it in books, because it existed in the liminal space between books, and classrooms, and hundreds of hours of poring over fragments. It existed only in his head and was woven deeply into his heart. But now he had limited access to his hidden treasures.

I moved from my seat to the chair next to him. I placed my hand on top of his shoulder, and said, "Don't worry about it, we got you." A young black man's slang words to an older white man that said "we will hold you up." I told him I would find someone to finish the semester and asked if he had any suggestions for teachers from the many students he had taught over the years. I thanked him for his wonderful work and who he is to the school and to students. Frank exposed a truth that is there at the beginning of the scholarly journey. Attention is always what we cultivate *together*, and carry with and for each other in hope of its unending.

. . .

Designing for attention, however, depends on another design: affection.

My loves are clear and out in the open. I love books and ideas and talking about them endlessly, deep into the night, or early in the morning with cups of coffee in the bright light of a new day, or, equally pleasurable, in the gray skies of a wintry noon. I love theology, all of it. I love African American studies, all of it. I love other fields as well, sociology, anthropology, geography, literary studies, and others. I love the ideas of a number of people, and I love them as much as it is possible to love those who are distant to you in time, space, or the contours of life. But I did not always name my loves so openly because in the academy affections are feared because affections have been forced. We live in the wake of a decision to limit loves, directing their flow in only one direction—away from nonwhite flesh and toward the European.

. . .

I remember my mistake. It came suddenly and at the worst possible place—in public. It was a hastily called town hall meeting, a divinity school community meeting where we, the chief administrators—the dean, the dean of student life, and me, the academic dean—would listen to the concerns and pain of black students and others who felt the school was not doing enough to address the racially hostile environment of the school. We listened as students told their stories of being disrespected, of not having their voices or ideas or sensibilities honored in the texts they were required to read, in the worship that was planned for the whole community, or in the sensibilities of ministerial formation that remained painfully white and relentlessly Eurocentric. I listened but I didn't. I knew these stories. I had lived them and was yet living them. I decided to step into this deep water of disrespect and try to pull people out, keep them from drowning, although I myself was not a strong swimmer.

I was tired, very tired. Long staff meetings and long hours listening carefully to those same students, one by one: all of this had weakened the patience that kept my frustration walled off from my words and actions. Tiredness erodes patience like water running continuously against a wall—forming a crease, then a hole, and finally breaking through. I got up to speak and I spoke eagerly about all the wonderful things to love in this school, the things to learn and to do and to experience (as if they did not know this). Then I spoke harshly and against the grain of student feeling, not denying their pain, but demanding they see the good, see what we were doing, what I was doing to change things. I was completely right in what I was saying but completely wrong in saying it. They could not hear me because I could not hear them in the pain of forced affections that performed searing disrespect.

As I spoke, I saw it in their faces—the look of the betrayed, of hope drained by an all-too-familiar reality, the black melancholy of the academy. The more I tried to explain myself, the deeper their faces showed betrayal. I stopped before I finished and returned to my seat defeated, and waited for the judgment. It came swiftly. From that day forward, those students who heard my voice in that meeting trusted it no longer. When they saw me in the hallways, they offered me that plastic greeting reserved for white people they did not trust. Their words to me were always guarded, restrained, separated from their animating passion. Worse yet, I became for them a transparency, someone to look through to see the machinations of white power and the desires of white men to ensure their silence and control. I was no longer a brother in arms but a tool to be used to get what they wanted.

I did want to be used, not as a manipulated or manipulating tool, but as someone who imagined he was facilitating affections—the love of things academic and the joy of conversations. I did not understand yet that affections cannot be formed on top of affections that have been forced and that the theological academy exists on a mountain of the bones of forced affection.

. . .

That forced affection grew out of a white aesthetic regime that circulated and still circulates ideas of the true, the good, the beautiful, the noble, the insightful, the penetrating, the transcendent, and the full range of human existence around the white body. As white colonial settlers built their worlds, they pulled native peoples into their world of aesthetic evaluation, connecting wide varieties of people across vast distances in a shared judgment not endemic to their forms of life. Together they would be taught what a beautiful dress looks like, what magnificent architecture looks like, the difference between good and bad wine, what are a good cigar, a proper pair of shoes, classic clothing, proper speech, correct writing, beautiful comportment, excellent music, proper dance, real art, and much more, and all of this woven into a vision of intellectual formation and moral development that found this white aesthetic essential for that pedagogical work. Indigenous peoples were taught these things in the process of building and sewing and cooking and planting and fixing and maintaining these things. They learned to value what was held up as more valuable than their lives. They were forced to configure the good of life around these goods. What does it mean to have your life always compared to that which has been made (by your actual blood, sweat, and tears) to be greater than your life, for example, this crop, that section of railroad, this ship, this plantation, that government building, this dam, and so on?

It meant an uneasy relationship with the true, the good, and the beautiful, especially when formed in the mind of the master class. (It also meant an uneasy relationship to institutions, which we will explore in the next chapter.) Although native peoples were chained to this white aesthetic, it did not mean that their creativity was chained. They indeed brought their own aesthetic judgments to the built environments and the master-made world pressed upon them, and they made things different and often made things better. The modern world formed in the bricolage of native worlds collided and collaborated with the old world of Europe, and together they formed the cultural baroque, something new and unanticipated.[5] Yet this reality of shared agency and shared creativity was occluded by a white aesthetic regime that refused to share the world of meaning and purpose with those outside the old world of Europe or the colonial West as well as their colonialized subjects.

Theological education in the West gloried in this refusal, and took as its task forming people who would embody this white aesthetic regime as fundamental to performing a gospel logic and a Christian identity. Western education is designed within a forced affection, shaped to take all of us on a journey of cultural addition—add to the great European masters other thinkers who are not white or male but who approximate them, add to the great European artists other artists who are also great like they are, add to the eternal wisdom and universal insights of Europe the wisdom of other peoples that resemble them. Add these nonwhite others as embroidery to frame a picture, or spices to season a dish.

Many scholars of color responded and still respond to this forced affection with a commitment to engage in theological conversation and form intellectual and aesthetic visions primarily from the voices, knowledge, and wisdom of their own peoples. The aim is clear: find a way to love. I have, however, met many nonwhite intellectuals in my career within and outside the academy who don't love their own peoples' ways of knowing or what they know. Designs of attention and affection have rendered them profoundly skeptical of both expandable founts of knowledge and expandable loves. Yet the terms of struggle here are still caught in a tragic design. The lie that started this flawed design was an exclusion used to organize love. Too many faculty and staff members of theological schools live unaware of that exclusion.

Theological education was created because people made choices to believe this and not that, to seek to understand this and shun thinking about that, to listen and learn from these teachers and to reject those teachers. Education itself does not exist without choices, difficult and sometimes painful choices that demand sacrifice, sometimes rejection, and sometimes persecution and death. Theological education that forgets this will cease to be on solid ground in its work. So an exclusion is necessary, but not the one often presented. The exclusion that began theological education was the choice to find our way to the crowd. We choose to listen to the Jewish rabbi, shunned by many of his own people, feared by the religious leaders, and watched by the Roman authorities. We choose him because we want something from him or we simply want him. This is an exclusion that aims toward a new reality of affection and learning, a learning of God's ways with other peoples, a learning of God's love for people we did not believe we could love and be loved by.

How do we design intellectual affection in the troubled spaces of forced affection? How do we escape the exclusionary logic that yet organizes love of learning? Theological education has always been a very difficult site at which to imagine answers to these questions because we have aligned the design of forced affection with the work of teaching toward or against theological orthodoxy. Another quiet war rages in theological schools and between theological schools where faculty line up their intellectual loves with their desire to instill their particular vision of orthodoxy or their desire to form students in a theological radicalism that they believe will free us from the problems of orthodoxy.

.   .   .

I remember Pam and Robert. They were fourth-year doctoral students in theology, assisting a senior professor in teaching the introduction to Christian theology course. Pam and Robert represented conflicting approaches to their work, and neither was following the approach of the senior professor as faithfully as they should have, which is how and why I got involved. The senior professor gave doctoral students significant freedom in supplementing the required reading with texts that they thought might be helpful to the students in covering the specific topics of the course. This is a great idea if you have schooled your doctoral student assistants in how to perform expanding love.

This was, however, too much freedom for Pam and Robert. Robert wanted to draw the students into a deeper appreciation of the problems of God language and the significance of extra-canonical texts and theologically heretical traditions for expanding visions of God. His supplemental readings reflected his dissertation interests. Pam countered with texts that explored biblical theologies and that grounded orthodox theological vision in Scripture, which reflected her dissertation interests.

The students were completely lost, and Pam and Robert had completely lost sight of the students. What was intended as discussion sessions turned into minilectures, where they presented their materials, and if any time was left (which there almost never was), they would comment on the readings the professor had assigned. Worse was the way Pam and Robert treated the students. They rarely asked the students questions or engaged them in what they were thinking. Not once did they explore the contours of faith and the structures of belief already present in the students. Nor did they bring the students into any meaningful engagement with the professor's lectures or the assigned readings. And when it came time for grading assignments, Pam and Robert evaluated the students on how well they understood their particular ways of approaching theology.

. . .

Teaching toward an orthodoxy or toward an antiorthodox orthodoxy is not in fact the problem; it is the exclusionary logic that attends these efforts that turns theological studies into a dismal science, draining it of the surprises of love. Designing for intellectual affection requires a discerning love that knows how to perform an exclusion that does not isolate but opens toward more intense listening and learning from one another, but that kind of design, like a good design for attention, also requires that we reckon with a third complex form of design: resistance.

✤

Resist the devil and he will flee from you.
Of course, you need to know the devil
to resist him.

✤

. . .

I remember Cevan. He found his way to see me. He was halfway through his master of divinity program, exactly 1.5 academic years in and 1.5 academic years until the finish line. At the beginning, he complained loudly, "I hate this place. I am not accepted here." He was Pentecostal—a young black Pentecostal man, shaped in COGIC light and grace (that is, by the Church of God in Christ denomination). He had gone through his first Bible courses, his first taste of higher criticism, the science of the text; gone through his church history, his first taste of the strangeness of his faith; gone through some theology and danced in complex thought; gone through late-night conversations with those he saw as suspect saints. He still did not belong here at divinity school, as far as he was concerned, but belonging was now a wider question, so deep that he was drowning in it.

"I have never preached. Never accepted by my pastor, Elder . . . (It does not matter)." I understood what he was not saying. It was my story too. I never preached in my home church under the pastor who watched my growing. I was too strange. But this is Cevan's story. Cevan was too strange. Cevan came to me because it was time to tell me. "I have never kissed a woman, but I have kissed a man." He said to me what is often said in the middle of the divinity school journey. This truth is often called forth in the presence of those who look for God, to think after God, and follow after divine desire.

"I am thinking about switching from the MDiv to the MTS (master of theological studies)." What he was actually saying was this: "I am very afraid now and I am thinking about switching from the degree program that says I am going to the church and be a pastor to the degree program that says I want to think about God and desire God but I must find a different place where I can belong." My question in response was simple: Why?

He cried. I cried.

My words after the tears were puny. I said to him, don't give up on the church, your church, my church, any church. In those years, it pains me to say, I had no deep theological vision to allow him to claim both his love of God and his love of men as shared sites of celebration. (That vision was to come later.) But I did want him to stay in his faith and to take hold of hope. He left my office and stayed in the master of divinity program. But this was not the victory he longed for. And it was not the victory I longed for.

I went to hear his first sermon, his initial embodied yet disembodied proclamation. It was in a church like his own but not his own (the pastor of his home church still barring his entrance to the pulpit). He preached like the preacher, sounded and sung, stepped and shook, sweet sweat and beautiful praise. After the service, I thanked him for the word of God, in him. He spoke to me with full preacherly affect and voice, "Thank you, doc." Sadly, he continued to wear that affect and that voice long after the first sermon. He found his way of belonging.

. . .

He was so much more than the sermon and the preacher suit he wore allowed him to be. But this is the condition of so many who enter theological education. They yield to the resistance and are not guided in the work of cultivating their own.

Speaking, Tongues Out

Have you ever spoken in tongues?
Yielded your voice to the Holy Spirit

It is a matter of the body,
In longing, sheer need
Embodying the Midnight hour

It is so easy to do
But so hard to admit, saying "I need you, I . . . need
God, I need . . ."

Then from deep in your belly,
Your royal gut
The secret anguish, the private joy
Fills your mouth

Your thoughts scatter, they shatter
They enfold your words,
like embroidery around a cloth
the cloth is the strange sound-words you

Utter

They utter you, draw you into sound
turn you into a moan, render you a deep groan

You are in total control and controlled totally
This is Praise of the Living God, living in you,

The Spirit dancing in your need for God and more

Utterances . . .

This is faith easily made fear to a world bent toward control,
fear even of the faithful, fear even to the faithful
Such yielding, desiring bodies are dangerously vulnerable
To that host—preacher-pimps, scholar-pimps,
    obedience-pimps
To a self, afraid of its own desiring revealed in the speaking
    tongue,

But the world needs speaking tongues and tongues joined
    together
Until voices strange and familiar are heard together

Now for the first time and never a last time

❧

. . .

I remember Dr. Zachary, almost twenty years into teaching, scholarship, and academic fellowship, and still he worried. He had come out as a young man, before toleration formed or acceptance was a word, or his courage was recognized for what it was—a gift from God. Brilliant from the beginning, an ideal graduate student, a scholar's scholar, and someone committed to teaching. I met him in my early years of teaching and our friendship grew. He taught at a wonderfully progressive school and was a strong voice on his faculty for LGBTQAI students, but he still worried. He worried about backlash, backtracking, gains lost, and the many places in this world where people like him were not safe, were in danger, and were being killed by a wide assortment of hands. I was invited to his school to lead the faculty in a workshop on teaching, and I did not want to go, because I knew what I would find out about Zachary and his classroom.

Zachary was raised in a lily-white town where black and brown and Asian peoples were coincidentally by practice absent, made so by housing prices, redlining, and other strategies of avoidance, strategies that also marked Zachary's formal education, both in college and in graduate school. Unfortunately those strategies had formed in Zachary, making him white down to the bone. The progressive school that he served was changing. A demographic wave was hitting the school and shifting the terrain from predominately white students to predominately black and brown and Asian students, precisely the kind of people Zachary had been formed to avoid at all cost, precisely the kind that Zachary had learned about through rumor and stereotype and half-baked books and raw comments by his many intellectual mentors.

Zachary was in a perfect storm. Zachary created a perfect storm. I had met students who had graduated from Zachary's socially progressive school, each having survived his required courses. They learned a lot but they had to work for it. But this was not the kind of work that anybody should need to do. Now, alone in a room filled with nonwhite students of this school, gay, straight, trans, queer, and more, I heard it in surround sound: Zachary's classroom was a place filled with very sharp eggshells, and students were afraid to step in any direction. Every lecture, every conversation, every answer to any question carried the feel of an inquisitor, looking for people who would dare to take him back to silence, to hiding, to struggle. Zachary has merged his strategies of resistance to his strategies of avoidance, which turned his classroom into quicksand. He kept his students at his beginning.

Most of them responded in the only way they imagined was available to them: they resisted. They whispered that he was a racist. But in that closed-door meeting with the black man from far away, they said it loudly and clearly. That broke my heart. The students learned to show respect in public but to resist in private, and that resistance carried no pedagogical health, no healing balm.

They deserved better, and Zachary was better than what he showed in his classroom. As was our custom, whenever we were together we shared a nightcap, a bit of libation to end a long day and renew friendship. Sitting at a table, he asked me, "So what did the students have to say? We have a lot of conservative students now." I did not want to test the cords, jump hard on this floor, for fear that something might break. I said, "They are not that conservative. They are struggling to feel heard here." That was all I said.

This was less the coward in me and more the tiredness. I knew Zachary's undone work in learning about his whiteness, the thought of which exhausted me, and I knew his raw, tender resistance to homophobia, which frightened me. Maybe I should have spoken to his resistance, trusting that the years of friendship had placed me deep inside his safe space where my words, even strongly offered, would carry a measure of comfort. But I realized that his resistance needed not just a pastoral intervention but also a communal restructuring, neither of which I could offer alone. I finished sipping and aimed myself toward my room.

. . .

Theological education is also about resistance. It is the seed from which may grow beautiful habitation or from which may grow mind-bending captivity. Yet how do you design for intellectual resistance? This may be the most pressing question in theological education today, because we theological educators are failing miserably at precisely this—at imagining a form of resistance that builds community.

🌿

I will listen, but I am not hear
You will speak, but you are not here-ing
You here me—putting me in my place
But this is not my place, it belongs to
those not wanting escape, me

DESIGNS

I am gone, my inside outside already
searching to hear where I am heard
as I listen.

❦

•   •   •

I remember Maximillian and Beatrice. They came to us as already accomplished students, having graduated near the top of their class in their respective schools. Maximillian had graduated from a historically black men's college in the South (US), and Beatrice from a women's college in the North (US). They were each poised, beautifully self-possessed, clear, decisive, courageous—and utterly unteachable.

They were not the first students from their respective schools who were this way; indeed, others (although by no means the majority of students) coming from these schools shared this problem. Maximillian and Beatrice, however, were special. Each of them had the power to draw people together, to organize and execute plans. Maximillian quickly became the president of the Black Seminarians' Union and the graduate student liaison to the black cultural center on campus and the organizer of the Black Graduate Student Alliance. Beatrice just as quickly became the student director of the Women's Center in the divinity school and a graduate assistant to the director of the university's women's studies program. Some faculty members held them up as models because they talked in exactly the ways those faculty members wanted students to talk. Other faculty members gave them lots of space, accepting their papers and listening to their speeches, always recognizing that these were the words and ideas that they inhabited while in college and were simply repeated to us.

Maximillian and Beatrice recognized each other's talents but also saw each other as opposition. That opposition grew as they engaged each other in classroom skirmishes until their antagonism toward each other grew beyond the bounds of the classroom.

Beatrice struck first. She organized a big conference with powerful speakers, each taking aim at gender oppression in various forms of Christianity and other religions but with a special focus on sexism and homophobia in the black church and an even tighter focus on black male leadership in the black church. Maximillian countered with a huge conference of his own with local and national speakers who brought searing critique against white privilege, and who focused on the intersectional oppression of black women, and with a special focus (as he announced in his opening comments) on "the problem of the white woman for black liberation." Beatrice surmised that Maximillian was aiming his comments at her, and so she made public comments directly aimed at him. Students lined up behind these leaders, and we had a very serious problem on our hands.

So I invited Maximillian and Beatrice to meet with me and the dean of students to discuss this matter. It did not go well. They ignored us deans and argued intensely, with us watching. They were articulate, insightful, and remarkably tone-deaf to each other. Listening to them, I was reminded of a story that the poet Toi Derricotte told in her book *The Black Notebooks*, of two students, a white woman and a black man, who got into a very painful and hurtful argument in front of the class. She said,

Once they were standing together, and I felt something so alive between them. I wanted them to go to bed with each other, to make love, for all of us.[6]

I felt a similar sentiment as I listened to these future leaders. I wanted them to take off their exquisite armor forged in the heat of years of their predecessors' struggles and touch each other for just a moment and see and feel a new kind of shared strength, and then see the possibilities of a new configuration of armor that they could wear together, forming a different kind of resistance that could build something.

. · .

The man who designed this wins too often. He wins because he has formed a design that designs attention, affection, and resistance, all directed toward achieving a compelling outcome, to cultivate the man who serves. The man who serves is too often mistaken for Jesus, but he is not Jesus.

"For the Son of Man came not to be served but to serve, and to give his life a ransom for many." (Mark 10:45)

A single life has been ransomed for the many. Jesus is the one who offers his body to create a space for communion with God, a joining space. This is God serving. The man who serves, in profound contrast, ransoms the many for the one. This man is a quiet tyrant, who, enamored with his own abilities, imagines the good he can do in the world and then evaluates and organizes people according to their usefulness in fulfilling his dreams. This "man" who serves (who can also be a woman) dreams the dreams of a master.

When the master returns
I will tell him, he did not win
even if I am not sure I believe that.
I will tell him that they are better servants
than their perfectly damaged obedience showed today.
He will probably laugh at me and say
"They are mine."
I know they are not. Even if they don't know it,
until he returns to end this master.

The deepest desire that should drive our educational designs is to cultivate people who serve, but that requires us forming them in a vision of people being formed into a people. Such vision articulates servant leadership through the desire to be a place of communion and in so doing to follow our savior in forming Jesus space. This Jesus space draws people to flourishing life together and to a work of building together. But building what? The answer is not what but where—they build around his body, they build against death, and they build toward a place of gathering that will never end.

3

Buildings

The creature builds.

All education is inside this truth.

The creature builds as God the Creator builds. The building of the creature must find its way into the building of the Creator or it builds toward death.

All theological education is inside this truth.

If we are willing to yield to the Spirit of God, God will draw us and our work of building into the building of God. But sometimes we must abandon what has been built in order to enter God's building work, and sometimes we must tear down what we have built in order to follow God in building toward life, and sometimes God can take what we have built toward death and turn it toward life.

All this is the work of edification and all of it is a struggle.

A few years ago, I was invited to Wheaton College in Illinois in the United States to give a lecture for an art exhibition. The art was a set of prints depicting African American worship and life that had been found in the Billy Graham Center Museum archives. The majority of the prints, some dating back to the (US) Civil War, were produced by white artists. There was one picture in particular that stayed with me, haunting me.

This image was in the *Illustrated London News*, published December 5, 1863.[1] On page 574 of the magazine is the following description, in part under the title "Slaves at Worship on a Plantation in South Carolina."

Slaves at worship on a plantation in South Carolina. Family Worship in a Plantation in S.C. *Sacred Arts Collection, Special Collections, Buswell Library, Wheaton College, IL.*

> *The owner of a cotton plantation, South Carolina [near Port Royal], is with his wife and children, engaged in Divine worship, surrounded by his slaves in a state of almost patriarchal simplicity. In the character of the negro as developed in the Slave States of America the two most marked features are his capacity for strong attachment and fidelity to his master when kindly treated and his susceptibility to religious influences. . . . The "incumbent" was an intelligent old house servant, a slave. He could read, but not write; and his extempore sermons . . . were characterized by strong good sense and a certain rude native eloquence, often rising to the dignity of pathos, and admirably adapted to the comprehension and temperament of his audience.*

What the writer and illustrator saw in this scene was not what I saw and certainly not what I felt. I felt these slaves. I felt the absurdity of this event as though it was an absurdity I shared in. One can see the absolute exhaustion of these slaves sitting in worship at the site of their life of forced labor. There are no smiles in this worship—only exhausted faces with eyes that express a truth I can see and feel even in an illustration and even across more than 150 years.

Here sits the master at the narrative center of this image, a presence so big that it dwarfs everyone else. He sits looking out at no one in particular with a posture that suggests both surveillance and avoidance. His suit of clothing is all in place. His Bible (or book) is closed.

He is not looking and certainly does not seem to be listening to the preacher with any seriousness. But he is being seriously observed. The slaves around him cannot ignore his presence, and the slaves who sit directly behind him see only him—no preacher, no worship, only the slave master. They stare at his back like prisoners watching a guard or detainees watching their torturer. But this is plantation worship. This is also the racial paterfamilias. "Paterfamilias" is an ancient term born of slavery in the Greco-Roman world that refers to a social system of rule formed around the body of the father-master as the fount from which flowed the life and logic of a social order.[2]

This worship service is the embodiment of the *racial* paterfamilias, that is, the rule of the plantation father over the family and of the master as the organizing center of domestic and public life. This plantation service also gestures to the biblical household codes and its domestic order: master–mistress (wife)–

children–slaves/animals. The mistress with daughter and son is positioned in the illustration near the body of the preaching slave, but no closer to his actual condition. The slave master's son is positioned directly below the pulpit, seemingly inside the pulpit itself. The son is in fact inside this churchly plantation logic and inside a trajectory that will bring him in time to the position of his father. Indeed, the son stares out in almost exact imitation of his father.

Maybe this plantation worship in the small chapel on the plantation was staged for the illustrator. It was, after all, 1863—in the midst of the Civil War. Maybe the melancholy on the faces of the slaves concealed their impatience with an emancipation that was within reach, just beyond the plantation and present in the sounds of battles that certainly they could hear. Even if this "state of patriarchal simplicity" was staged, the faces of the slaves spoke the real. They were inside a building that spoke death—not simply the small chapel building of this plantation worship, but also this constrained slaveholding worship itself, and not only this, but also the form of Christianity that made it all possible.

I can see in their faces the horror of it all: one young man buries his head in his hand, another person stares at the preacher

as if in mourning, and not one black woman in the illustration looks impressed by this event. This is not boredom, because even boredom shows life. This is something else—a slow death in a slave obedience. None of my musings can be verified, but I hold them to be true.

Why or how this image found its way into the Billy Graham Center Archives at Wheaton is a mystery. I could imagine an eye formed to see this as a pleasurable and even hopeful image—a plantation at worship, master and mistress with their "extended family" in worship of God. Yet the horror and absurdity of this image are bound up in the order of it. This is an institution—church as institution, slavery as institution, white supremacy as institution, all woven together. But my deepest torment at looking at this image radiates from the preacher in the pulpit.

I would like to think that this preacher was engaged in what Henry Louis Gates famously articulated as "signifying," that is, a slave who spoke words that would be approved by the master and slaveholding society but would also be understood by slaves as coded words that camouflaged rebellion, revolution, and plans for escape.[3] I dream that his gospel eloquence belied a seething

hatred of the institution of slavery and a desire to destroy the very arrangement within which he stood. But the faces of the slaves don't suggest such a linguistic stratagem. Instead I imagine that this slave preacher is an enslaved preacher proclaiming a gospel useful to this institution—church, slavery, whiteness.

All theological education in the Western world is haunted by this illustration: a plantation at worship and an enslaved preacher.

Even places and settings and people involved in theological education far removed from the history of the slaveholding United States are implicated in this scene, yet inhabiting a building formed with this same enslaving design: an ecclesial reality inside a white patriarchal domesticity, shaped by an overwhelming white masculinist presence that always aims to build a national and global future that we should all inhabit.

The slave legacy of Western education, especially theological education, is lodged deeply in our educational imaginations. It set our work of formation inside a pedagogy of the plantation. Plantations throughout the colonial world were always about more than just cultivating crops and preparing goods and services to be exported and imported through the known world.

Plantations were also about cultivating leadership and establishing a social order necessary for promoting commerce and civilization.[4]

Slavery taught us how to build.

It taught us how to build a home, how to build a church, how to build a school, and how to build a person. Slavery took a theological truth—that the creature builds—gave thanks for it, broke it into pieces, and forced us to eat the stones.

These are the stones that the builders did not reject.

I knew a dean who would say *almost daily* that the church and the (theological) academy are not the same thing, nor should we confuse the two—the church has one function and the academy has another function. This is strange wisdom that recognizes a fact but not a truth, especially not a racial truth. The church and the academy, theological or otherwise, have been bound to the same whiteness since the advent of colonialism. Both have been made to aim at a work of building an institutionalizing life that lay in the racial world like sunbaked mud that carries ancient power to grow bitter roots and poison herbs.

Teaching Threshold

I have, countless times, entered to joy and entered again to
 pain, exited in sweet relief
until once again, I enter my life—to enter, again and again,
 always finding there in the
room new old faces, appearing quickly through the door,
 and then I, this black body, am in
front of them speaking, looking, listening to their bodies. It
 appears freshly—the threshold
they may enter in as they pass from then to now to new
 again, always crossing, as I cross,

into the room-filled-white to the opening to another thresh-
    old to the life-filled-room that
would allow them to exit, if they wished, this white death
    and enter life and then another
entering again, if they wished, away from more white death
    and into more life until only
One threshold remains—around these thresholds—into the
    still standing eternity.

What is an institution?

An institution is a sustained work of building. It is a joining aimed at eternity where people, seeking to create the new, commit themselves to a powerful repetition that they hope will never end. Institutions, especially educational institutions, always express the work of building:

The buildings we inhabit, spatially, architecturally, electronically, and conceptually,

The building projects we want to sustain and the legacies we want to maintain,

The individuals we want to cultivate and the forms of cultivation we prefer,

The way of life we want to commend and the ways of life we want to discourage.

We theological educators have never reckoned sufficiently with the racial character of institutional life in the colonial West, and because of this failed reckoning we have never fully understood how distorted has been our work of building. We are caught in a distorted institutionalizing practice that hinders life-giving institutional performance and that thwarts the development of a healthy institutional personality. To imagine how we go from distorted practice to life-giving performance in the formation of healthy institutional personality is the goal of this chapter.

Buildings

*Can you dream institutionally or
does that sound oxymoronic—
too much like mixing joy and task?*

The distorted institutionalizing practice I have in view here is not a single practice, a single behavior, or even a single pattern of action, but a practice energized by whiteness that enables practices that always bend toward the racial paterfamilias and reinforce the racial character of our institutional life.

The journalist Ellis Cose, in his classic book *The Rage of a Privileged Class*, tells a story that has nothing to do with theological education but has everything to do with the racial character of so much of Western institutional life. He was interviewing a very successful black corporate lawyer about black middle-class rage over the relentless disrespect and what we would now call the microaggression that characterize much of black professional life, in response to which the lawyer told him this story:

> [The black lawyer] arrived at the office an hour or so earlier than usual and entered the elevator along with a young white man. They got off at the same floor. No secretaries or receptionists were yet in place. As [the black lawyer] fished in a pocket for his key card while turning toward the locked outer office doors, his elevator mate blocked his way and asked, "May I help you?" [The black lawyer] shook his head and attempted to circle around his would-be helper, but the young man stepped in front of him and demanded in a loud and decidedly colder tone, "May I help you?" At this, the older man fixed him with a stare, spat out his name, and identified himself as a partner, whereupon his inquisitor quickly stepped aside. [The black lawyer's] initial impulse was to put the incident behind him. Yet he had found himself growing angrier and angrier at the young associate's temerity. After all,

he had been dressed much better than the associate. His clients paid the younger man's salary. The only thing that could have conceivably stirred the associate's suspicions was race: "Because of his color, he felt he had the right to check me out."[5]

The young white man's actions captured a truth of institutional life in the colonial West where the presumptive possessiveness of whiteness imagines its central role in building and sustaining ordered life. This young man was being a white master, not as a person but as an institutional personality, a masculinist personality that usurps responsibility for the well-being and protection of an institution. He enacted the one who must control the space and orders small worlds.

. . .

I remember Sheldon. He was now in his fourth year on faculty at his school. He thought things were going well at his school. They were going well for him but not for many of those colleagues who had to work closely with him. I had known Sheldon since his graduate-school days—intellectually quick, politically savvy, and very ambitious—he wanted to go far and high in the profession. The job market was not kind to him. Three years in and no job, and then a break: there was a job opening soon to be announced in a seminary. His doctoral director went to work convincing the school president to hire Sheldon without an extensive search. He got the job. It was a low-level faculty position with low-level administrative responsibilities.

His faculty colleagues were a diverse group that included two senior African women, one newer Latina, an African American man who had been at the school for fifteen years, and an African American woman academic dean, all of whom I knew very well, just as well as I knew Sheldon. From the very beginning Sheldon claimed what did not exist—his right to lead. He chaired every committee, especially all those he was not designated to chair. He explained the best way to do everything in every field, every class, every administrative operation, and every event. He listened to his colleagues of color like a fish rides a bike and ignored any suggestions that he might need more emotional intelligence. I had heard over the years about his behavior, but it was not until I visited the school that I saw the real problem: the president respected and liked Sheldon and so did some of the other white men and women. The faculty of color did not. At all.

This was not a case of classic white male cronyism because Sheldon was capable of leading. This, however, was something far more sinister than the machinations of a "good old boys" fraternity. Sheldon positioned himself as the one who bore the institution's ethos in his body, and the president found it easy to imagine that to be the case. During my visit, I could sense what the faculty of color had already sensed—that Sheldon wanted the academic dean's position and then the presidency of the school. The faculty of color had all seen this movie before—a young ambitious white man or woman enters the institution and quickly moves up the ranks and returns the school to a past that person thinks is a future.

.   •   .

Ambition was not the problem here, nor was his wanting to be in leadership, and it was certainly not his enthusiasm for a school's mission. The problem was that Sheldon claimed a place that conjured a ghost—a white master who sees everyone and listens to no one—and he thereby yielded to a spirit that afflicts and oppresses institutional life in the West: the racial paterfamilias and the household order of master, mistress, children, and slaves/animals/other property.

❧

What does leadership feel like? What is its taste? How is its touch? What does it see and how does it hear? Can you smell the scent moving through the hallways, filling each room with a presence that captures the senses and moves to the mind? Is it an old smelling, touching, tasting, seeing, hearing, or is it a new in an old or a new with an old—an old smell but a new feel, or an old taste but a new sound—or must it be new altogether to be leadership,

so that a new affection
and a new comfort
and a new way
to be "the always"
captures us?

The racial paterfamilias spirit haunts all Western institutions, but its presence in educational spaces and especially the theological academy lives close to the surface, ready to reassert itself. That spirit lies so close to our institutionalizing practice because it was born of Christianity in its colonialist form, moving and feeling itself in the power to dream a world well organized and running efficiently like a plantation where bodies are organic machines and profit begets more profit.[6]

Very few organizations today would image themselves as haunted by the racial paterfamilias because they do not know or sense its ancient power that is always present with us. That, however, is a tragic mistake. Like a father always looking to form a son, the racial paterfamilias spirit forms in the psychic and affective spaces between efficiency and profit, between desired order and desired influence. It seduces ambition and changes vision so that people are seen as tools for use, slaves implicitly, but never acknowledged as such out loud—important, yes, valuable, yes, even honored on a temporal plane of existence that touches only their efforts and never their bodies. Their bodies carry a shelf life.

The racial paterfamilias, in order to be seen and in order to be thought, must be felt, and many people of color know it because we feel it—that sense of an old sorrow, of life between an old master dying and a young master coming to life through power. It is like a sick-smelling scent riding in on a wind blowing

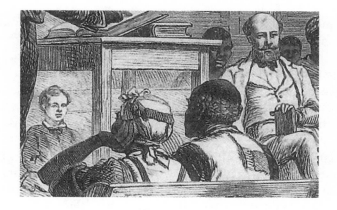

from a past and reaching toward a future. And we who exist in the middle-present—smelling and sensing—carry a melancholy undeserved and unwanted.

Many scholars of color carry this melancholy through the academy. They feel the forming of young masters (both men and women) and the yielding of a place (a school, or a department, or an organization) to an affective reality of white masculinist concern and longing.

. . .

I remember Mark Eric. He was an academic dean living in the midst of his own Greek tragedy. I had been invited to lecture at his school, and he asked me to come in a little early to help him think through a crisis at the school. It involved an African American woman faculty member and the school's new president, who was also a woman. I knew both the faculty member and the president very well. Nadea, the African American woman scholar, was amazing—a highly trained New Testament scholar and liturgist and also an accomplished sculptor. She had incredible creativity and energy, but her previous institution exploited her badly, using her work, her image, her enthusiasm for teaching and scholarship, and her love for the students and the black community to promote itself without properly compensating her. She came to this new school, Mark Eric's school, because the previous president made her a promise of a new start, where she would have a center shaped around her work, a reduced teaching load, and an assistant to help with her many projects. Although she was not a member of the founding denomination of the school, he told her the school would build its future with her and her work, so she uprooted and came.

Timing is everything, and this was a bad time to uproot. The school hit a serious financial crisis due to serious mismanagement and a president's constant mistakes over many years. Now he was out and a new president was in place. Janice, the new president, had been an academic dean herself. For many years she had served as the only woman on a senior administrative staff at a seminary, working in the thick fog of a white masculinist ecology, but now the air had cleared and she was the president of a seminary that was well established but also in deep financial trouble. The board demanded two things of their new president: make the school solvent again by making the necessary cuts, and align the school more clearly with its denominational identity. Janice was on the same page as the board, and she was eager to prove that she was the right choice to lead the institution.

Nadea settled into her new school, but it felt like the place she had just left, only worse. Two years in and no center, no assistant, and a rocky relationship with Janice. Mark Eric wanted Nadea to "understand" this difficult situation that no one had anticipated. He wanted her to be a comrade in arms with Janice against "those forces" that were trying to undermine her presidency because she was a woman. In turn, Mark Eric advocated consistently for Nadea but not strongly enough to get Janice to think inside the promises made to Nadea by her presidential predecessor whose name had now become a curse word. "He made extravagant promises that we cannot keep"—Janice's words rang in Mark Eric's ears every time he listened to Nadea's complaints.

Nadea had those extravagant promises in writing, which

meant that the time with the lawyers was approaching. Nadea did not want a litigious world to become her world. All she wanted was the promised place where she would build inside a building that honored her efforts and where she joined others in this good work. Neither Janice nor Mark Eric wanted to enter a litigious world either, and the public relations nightmare it would bring. But they did not want to build a world with Nadea.

🌿

I felt the old anger . . .

🌿

I tried to have empathy for Janice and Mark Eric but I did not, because they both knew better. Academic deans, most of us, know better. Nadea represented a different way of thinking, being, and doing the work of theological education. She was a profound moment of stretching for their institution. Janice and Mark Eric did not have the interest or patience necessary to think the future with Nadea, to sit with her and imagine together what her work could be even with their limitations and what sacrifices they could make for her even in their limitations.

There are times when schools and particular scholars don't align well, their lives and their visions moving in opposite directions. It takes a grace to see that and to have the courage to separate, if possible. But Janice and Mark Eric refused the process of discerning such knowledge and moved to stabilize an institutional identity that had already irrevocably changed because Nadea was there.

Nadea not only left the school, she also left the academy. She was exhausted. She came exhausted, and this new school not only took the last energy she had but stole her joy and emptied out her creativity. Janice narrated her leaving as collateral damage, a bad fit within the constellation of bad executive decisions made by the past president. Mark Eric operated in less denial and grieved Nadea's loss, but neither of them understood what they had done: they had turned the school into a plantation.

.   .   .

❦

So she told me that this would be the last time that she would listen to her heart. Too many disappointments, too many cuts of disrespect into her sensitive soul. She would leave this school, this thorn-crusted place, as soon as another job came open. She, fighting back tears, voice quivering, vowed to remain steady as she drove me to the airport at the end of my visit. I prayed while she talked. "God, please help her not to give up on her calling. Please, God, heal her. She is a fabulous teacher, you know this, God, one of the best I ever helped make it through the doctoral program. Don't let the crude bastards win in her, their voices finding a permanent home." I remembered my moment, my last time, and I prayed that this would be the last time she had a last time.

❦

Running an educational institution, and especially a theological institution, is a complicated business: it is exceedingly difficult to explain to an outsider all the factors that go into making decisions, and sometimes those decisions are made by the circumstances that bully us into places we would prefer not to go. But not all bullies are hated. Some are imitated because we see in them an efficiency and a clarity of action that fit the way we see the world, even if and especially if that world is not the world we want but simply the world as it is. To be reconciled to the way the world is can become a sick wisdom, one that imprisons us even as it allows us to function. That reconciliation to the givenness of a situation and to a way of being that constantly forms us toward an administrative acquiescence to the world is just as much feeling and sensing as it is thinking. We could call this nexus of feeling, sensing, and thinking the institutional unconscious similar to what Frederic Jameson called the political unconscious.

For Jameson, the political unconscious is the way the world in its relational density—politically, socially, economically—shows itself in the very things one would imagine are sequestered from such realities. In Jameson's concern, that would be literature imagined as far removed from the deep reflexes of those realities.[7]

The institutional unconscious of that nexus of feeling and thinking is not a bad thing. In fact, it is a wonderful thing, but under the wrong influences and pressures it can press us to accept the givenness of the world for the sake of efficiency and functionality. For us, that institutional unconscious is deeply infected with the racial paterfamilias, beckoning us with a tested and true seduction that promises to organize hopes and dreams, tactics and strategies toward the goal to build.

The feeling and sensing of the racial paterfamilias, however, remains a mystery to large portions of the academy, especially the theological academy and those who live down in the belly of a school where decisions are made, because it first requires entering fully into the affective reality of Western institutional life. There remains a legion of scholars and administrators who continue to hold a dualism of thought and feeling. The educational space in their way of thinking is a space of thinking, not feeling. Too many scholars believe in rigorous thinking and banished feelings, and they teach students that a thinking subject wars with a feeling subject.

So an institution that thinks itself makes sense to them, but an institution that feels itself does not. But institutions feel just as institutions think. To discern institutional thinking is also to explore institutional feeling. More specifically, it is to invite those who inhabit an institution to sense its comfort, its joy, and its energy aimed in a direction, even if it is the wrong direction.

. . .

I remember Margaret with my tears. She was a mature African American woman, having spent many years in the white corporate world. She came to seminary on the heels of a painful divorce, the culmination of a man's decision not to live with a preacher. She was clear about her calling and who she was. And she was simply magnificent—one of the best students to move through our master of divinity program. Some come this way, ready to lead, ready to pastor, ready to share in the anointing of the healer. As she approached graduation, a fantastic opportunity was on the horizon.

Her last semester I was approached by a large black Baptist church in the region, solidly stable in its life and progressive in its vision. They were looking for a freshly trained pastor, and they wanted my help. This was the rarest of the rare—a black church asking a divinity school academic dean about someone to pastor them. I thanked God, and went to work with them.

I listened carefully to their needs. I took several trips to them to meet and think and pray. I wanted to make sure they were worthy of Margaret and that she would be right for them. The answer was yes. This would be an answer to prayer—a wonderful black woman for a wonderful black church. She went and preached, and taught, and talked and talked. The congregation responded to her beautifully. The fit was great, and the world was right. The semester was drawing to a close and graduation was on the horizon and the decision for a pastor would soon be announced.

Days before graduation, I got the call. "Dr. Jennings, this is Deacon —— and I am here with the whole committee and we have you on speaker phone." Others spoke up, "Hey Brother Jennings, Hey Rev., Hey Doc." After good solid southern pleasantries, the deacon spoke up. "We wanted to tell you our decision for the pastor of our church. We are going to go with the brother, Reverend ——." They knew they had to call me because to decide and not tell me would add hateful to hurtful. And I was hurt, truly hurt.

They explained, but I was not listening. All I could do was be silent and cry. All that time—memo after memo of instruction on what to look for in a pastor, what questions to ask in the interview, what processes of discernment, examination, investigation to engage in—all of it turned to trash. I remember two of the women on the committee saying something about not being ready for a woman, and my head starting hurting.

I knew the brother they had chosen. Tall, mocha brown, deep

rich baritone voice, arresting smile, and only two weeks of divinity school education under his belt. He started at the divinity school and stopped after 1.5 weeks—too busy for this, he said. But he was an old-school churchman, with a familiar sound and a familiar way—a strong man who leads.

The racial paterfamilias knows no borders, respects no boundaries. It moves through institutions big and small, seen and unseen, and it lives wherever the design for a Christian-formed master lives, and that is everywhere Christians live. It would be a terrible mistake to imagine the racial paterfamilias only residing in majority white institutions and not where it wants to be, where it needs to be to form the feeling and thinking of institutional completeness—in bodies black and brown, in places and spaces called Asian, called indigenous, called native, called independent but dependent on an institutional practice that conceals an institutional unconscious: strong men (even if they are women) must lead. They must become masters.[8]

The next year, after my sorrow, the city-wide revival happened as it did every year, and I was asked again to bring greetings from the divinity school. The preacher was a black woman known for being a brilliant preacher, and she was a brilliant preacher. And she preached like a man, a very old man. The minister who was asked to do the altar call (which in the black Baptist revivalist tradition is the obligatory call to discipleship after the sermon) was the mocha-man, baritone brother, now one year into his new church. His opening comments were "The preacher preached. She preached just as powerfully as any man would've preached."

Absolutely.

. · .

❧

Student Sermon

Never done words
Like this

CHAPTER 3

I feel their eyes, joined to mine, we see vaguely into each
  other in
this artificial space.
I wrote out my words-feelings-fear-hope
Never ever worked this hard
For a graded word
Incline your ears and hear my prayer
I hear my voice in this sterile white space
Sound studio, sound studious, sounding student
Peers piercing my walls, sharing my anxiety
My turn into their turns
We each remember this is only a test
We are the real.

Each takes a hand at God
Speaking old-new, now new-old
All you all them—watching, listening to hear
Your soul, your heat
"Say it!"
"Stay right there"—though you really want to run
"When I think about the goodness . . ."
I want to run
"When I think about my life . . ."
I want to run
When I think about this space, a space meant to end con-
  fined spaces
I want to run, flee this space
It is not me, but it holds me.

Out on a limb, high enough to yet
See faces but too high for a safe fall
No choice but to take my voice and soar

The racial paterfamilias guides institutional unconscious into
a bad practice of assimilation. That is its greatest power: to as-

similate, not loudly, not through force of will or threat of life, but through the senses seductively trained until the truth is known like the sight of the wind through its effects, and then your voice is gone and you sound like the master even in your resistance to the master.

· · ·

I remember when Karen came to Lela's school, this small seminary inside a Christian world made up of Pentecostals and charismatics of many places and exhibiting times past, present, and future. Lela was the first black person on faculty, the first woman, the first one formed in Holy Ghost fire and burning intellectual light who claimed proudly this beautiful heritage, black and Pentecostal. Twenty-two years later, at this same school, she had become a serious war veteran living on the front lines of white (seminary) supremacy; hardened through battle, clear in both tactics and strategy, she had seen it all. Except for a Karen. Karen, the African American woman, was number two in the school, the one who would be the second after Lela's first. But Karen was no one's second.

Karen was shaped in a world deeply mixed, both by educational environment and by life. Her father was white British-Trinidadian, and her mother black American from the heart of Philly. Karen moved through worlds, white and black, with an ease Lela had never seen and could not quite understand. What Lela did not understand she sought to make understandable by correcting. Karen was an unwilling mentee.

I knew them both, and each had my ear. Lela wanted Karen to join her in battle against the institution: "Take up your weapon, woman, and fight beside me!" This was Lela's battle cry, unheeded by Karen. Karen did not want to copy the lines of hate and love, friend and foe, right and wrong exactly as Lela had drawn them.

Here is where the pain and trouble began. Lela soon made her tension with Karen about their skin: hers was dark, Karen's light; their minds: hers was clear, Karen's confused; their political vision: hers was diaspora nationalist, Karen's compromised; even their aesthetic: hers was of the mother land (Africa) and Motown, Karen's Euro/white American/poppish. None of this made sense until one imagined life inside the racial paterfamilias where people have a role, and if they resist that role then their existence is rendered unassimilable and useless.

Lela was trapped in the same institutional practice that she resisted: she had assimilated the institutional desire to assimilate—to turn people into tools, the leading edge against but also of exploitation.

There was a struggle at Lela and Karen's seminary against the whiteness that destroys, and there was a need for them to think together about institutional life, but the diseased institutional unconscious they lived in thwarted that thinking.

Lela knew the institution now in primarily one way: as the plantation constantly in the making. She had known it in other ways, including as a place of joy and satisfaction in teaching those students who respected her and journeying with those few colleagues who shared a Pentecostal faith reaching to become new. But after many years, those other ways of knowing weakened like tires worn down by use, until she could feel the road's every bump and texture, and she sensed in herself the panicked squeal of worn tires with every institutional turn.

Lela had been denied the opportunity to build in the institution and build with the institution. The school took her labor and denied her life. It watched her words and kept surveillance over her body, making sure she stayed one of them in thought and deed, and yet her colleagues and the administration never listened to her ideas or heeded her advice. She did not know how much more of this she could take.

Karen was new to this school's world, but she knew this racial world and she could see what the school's world had done to Lela and she vowed a distance. She would not enter in as deeply as Lela, and she would form her career only on the surface of the institution and never down in its inner workings.

.   .   .

This is the tragedy of distorted institutional practice built on a diseased institutional unconscious. It steals from people what God gives to every creature—the desire to build—and what the carpenter's son from Nazareth wants to give—the desire to build together.

We should call it institutional alienation—
the child conjured through the alchemy of whiteness.
It aims to cultivate us
through a plantation logic
that plots us all on a continuum
from slave to master.

There are, of course, people who for reasons too many to list here are not good workers, and some who are deviously destructive. They have made themselves agents of death through a bargain with destruction that they believe will give them institutional power. But this number of people is small, very small, and even then they are not the reprobate, not the shadow side of institutional election. Reprobates do not exist in this world that God has formed through love. Yet too many theological institutions and too many institutions in general seek to create reprobates. But this too goes back to the plantation.

Building the New Babel

Let's try this again, but now with noise
A cacophony of voices that none of us can control
We need that destroying God
Who made all of this happen
Threw away our plans and sat down in our midst

Chapter 3

You, God, speak to each of us
We can now only speak through You
To one another and understand
What and how to build with what stone which wood whose cloth
Whose hand which eye whose feet which arm every mind each hope
Climbing higher
Nothing will be wasted, no one will be thrown away
Then we will say to One as one
We have built together only what You wanted
What we desired to see
You in your home

❧

The task I hated most as a dean was terminating people (even the designation speaks of death, pressing me into the role of willful executioner). We live in a litigious society, so most institutions create a process of warnings, interventions, conversations, and documentation (like a staircase up to a hangman's noose) that allows them to terminate someone efficiently. But to have a careful process does not mean that an institution is careful with people. It just means that they don't want to be sued. To tell someone that they are not a good fit for an institution is to make a claim that needs deep context, and in my experience that context is often missing. I don't mean that educational institutions tend not to do due diligence in how they terminate staff or deny tenure or release workers or form severance packages. I mean that we who inhabit institutions often refuse to touch the deep colonial consciousness that flows like subterranean waters beneath us, so when we terminate, when we end a relationship with someone, we most often perform the master.

• • •

I remember Stella. She was eager to work in a divinity school, thrilled to be at a place where her faith and her work could openly embrace. The position for which she was hired was a step up for her, with several people reporting to her and she being asked to offer genuine leadership to the institution. Stella worked very hard, but her efforts always veered in the wrong direction. Her dedication was unfortunately coupled with an inability to hear the nuances of matters, which meant she worked like a bull in a china shop, breaking things as she attempted to fix things and damaging things that were working just fine. People struggled with her.

How long should we struggle with a person who is not doing an adequate job? Even to ask the question is a sign of grace through which we recognize that everyone deserves a struggle. No one should be cast away at the first sign of inadequacy, nor should someone be left to suffer in a position for which they are failing. But between quick cuts and tortured neglect there is holy time for prayer, for intervention, discernment, and hope.

The decision was made to terminate Stella, and that I should be the one to tell her the news. We talked at the end of the workday. She cried, I cried. This was not just the loss of a position for her, but to her mind she had failed in faith-filled service to God. My words of affirmation and clarification spoken in urgent repetition could not free her from this conclusion. After she left my office, I sat there heartbroken. A colleague came into my office afterward. He could see that I had been crying. Shaking his head in disapproving disgust, he told me that I was too sensitive and too nice to lead. And he could see that in my reluctance, my hesitancy to "lower the boom," as he said, that is, to fire people who needed to be let go.

.   .   .

He was expressing a sensibility that is familiar to anyone working in business or administration: one needs a focused coldness that can be deployed with precision when needed for the sake of the efficient operation and well-being of the institution. This is another piece of sick wisdom that denies the formative effects of cultivating such a skill.

That wisdom says there is a threshold one must cross in order to be aligned with an institution, to be a keeper of its light and a guardian of its life. One must be willing to see people as an obstacle when they become a complication that slows down the work of building and then move them out of the way—quickly and decisively.

This wisdom is ancient, formed well before colonialism, but its current colonial form announces a pedagogical function: it signals maturity, a maturity of whiteness, a form of masculinity, and even a kind of faith. It is the maturity that comes to the son-become-the-father and the one-(man or woman)-become-the-master because they can deal decisively with the help.

Thavolia Glymph, in her brilliant book *Out of the House of Bondage*, tells the powerful story of slave mistresses in the American South who carried the burden of running the slave household as an essential extension of the rule of the father-master. Fundamental to that responsibility was brutally subjugating slave women through constant violence. The mistresses, not the masters, were the primary source of violence against slave women as they sought to sustain the institution of slavery in and through their homes. The success of the husband as a slave owner depended on the slave mistress: in order to be the proper woman and wife, she had to perform the master perfectly.[9]

So much of the discussion about institutions and leadership misses this legacy. Many even long for the reassertion of master logics. Even in organizations that believe they have transcended this legacy through team building, power sharing, deep collaboration, open door policies, and practices that celebrate employees and listen to their ideas and concerns, the legacy yet lurks. It flows through the institutional unconscious like a virus, convincing too many that to commit to an institution is to commit to becoming the master. It also infects those who vow a distance from institution even as they live with it, having been convinced that surface institutional living is the only way to save one's life and keep one's humanity. I have known and yet know many a faculty or administrative colleague who keep a barbed-wire-encrusted concrete wall between their institution and their life and faith, especially if they work in theological contexts.

This distorted institutional practice of a Christian faith formed in colonial power calls to theological institutions as part of our mission to cast out this legion-forming demon—to end this practice first in our institutional homes and then to challenge it in a world that finds it useful because it promises a power to form a world in power.

I have covered a lot that bears summarizing before I go on:

The work of building has been damaged for us. Its truth and joy have been concealed from us through the cultivation logics of the colonial plantation and the institutionalizing practice it formed and inspired.

The colonial plantation was never just a place or a moment long past. It revealed to us the spirit of the racial paterfamilias, a seducing power that invites us into a form of cultivation aimed at building masters who desire to build, embodying self-sufficient masculinist form, and who carry a relentless vision of people as essential tools necessary for the work of building. Those who inculcate this masculinist persona are prepared to lead.

We cannot simply think our way into discerning the racial paterfamilias and its seductive cultivating power. We must feel it and think it, recognizing that institutions feel as they think and think as they feel. That nexus of thinking and feeling is the institutional unconscious. This is a good thing and needs to be honored and discerned in all institutions, because it is the reality that guides our administrative dreaming, planning, longing, and hoping.

The racial paterfamilias, however, wove itself into the institutional unconscious of educational institutions, and especially theological institutions, inviting us to sense through the cultivation logics of the plantation and whiteness the way the world actually is and to imagine how we could function efficiently and effectively in it.

The racial paterfamilias draws all of us toward an administrative acquiescence that would seduce us into believing that only two options for institutional practice exist: either move toward its affective vision of plantation-like efficiency and effectivity, or live in institutional alienation, always only on the surface of institutions in resistance and abiding suspicion.

Building, however, is a gift given to us by God. It is a doing that speaks our destiny, and it is inescapable. We build either toward life or toward death. But how do we know when our institutional practice is building toward life and not death? It takes a discernment that can see when institutional operations are moving in the right direction, spiraling up toward life and away from death. It takes a sensing of motions that are institutional operations, both subtle and exaggerated, that gesture toward either captivity or freedom, and of encouraging the motions that aim to form a place of life together. Too often we forget that institutions, especially educational institutions, as living realities build themselves freshly with every new generation. Like a body replacing cells, institutions can become new while expressing the same form, but even that form can be made something unanticipated—a place of new desire made visible in the world.

4

Motions

We live building
with the motions that
compose a living or a
dying

The work of building in education touches the deepest structures of personhood, moving its way through the sinews of hope and desire, longing and fear, all bound up in the irrepressible energy that forms at the intersection of teachers, students, and administrators. There at that meeting place, thinking and feeling and acting layer upon each other, spiraling up and down. Those spiraling motions never stop. Like the wind, they can be incredibly creative or dreadfully destructive. They can facilitate healing or harm. By spiraling motions, I am referring to the energy constantly unleashed by the actual daily operations of an educational institution. This chapter explores how we might reshape those spiraling motions toward life by reframing the daily operations of a school inside a new vision of edification. We urgently need a new vision of edification informing our daily work that builds people toward each other.

We are yet caught in an institutionalizing practice set in place by the plantation and the slave master. The spiraling motions of that practice seek to draw us deeper inside the cultivation of a particular kind of institutionalizing masculinist persona—the man builder, one who, even in the operations of a school, performs an isolating self-sufficiency.

Could self-sufficiency
be redeemed?
But who would want
such a thing?
Certainly not one who asked
Mary for life, or one
who needed friends along
the way of discipleship, or
one who called on an Abba-God, or
one who fell onto God's Spirit
like a limp body
in need of support just to
face the morning sun
or one who said, "This is my body and my blood,
eat me
because you need me in you."
Certainly not one who on a cross
killed the illusion of
self-sufficiency.

Theological educational institutions live in a spiraling wind that must be freed from the white master's motions by changing the motions—changing how we move into one another's lives, how we move back and forth from inside to outside, and how we move in radically new directions. The thicker words I use for these three changes in motion are "assimilation," "inwardness," and "revolution."

We need an assimilation that does not harm but heals. To assimilate is to be placed inside someone else's way of life and to follow in that way. It is like entering a house and living inside its structure. The house of theological education as well as all Western education was built to make us men, and we are yet haunted by *the motion to make us men*. This house of education formed a duplex—two kinds of habitation in the same house, one of master formation and the other of slave emancipation.[1] Both were inside this house of assimilation, and both aimed at moral formation. Master formation meant entrance into the racial paterfamilias through which indigenes would enter the European world of civilization and citizenship and thereby enter their humanity. This trajectory represented a marriage of ancient forms of Christian formation with modern colonialist logics, combining a civilizing impulse with a soteriological sensibility.[2] To save a soul was to educate a body, and to educate a body was to save a soul. There is something right about such a sensibility, but woven inside greed, theft, chauvinism, and whiteness, that sensibility became encrusted with a veneer of a strange morality that in effect made Western educational assimilation the reality of salvation. Education as master formation always moves toward an assimilation that hides as it assimilates, sending up the message that it is engaged in a moral formation that cultivates people into thoughtful subjects, excellent workers, and good and responsible citizens.

The other side of the house, however, held a different way of educating, one aimed at emancipation and at weaponizing learning. Without denying master formation, this way of educating sought tools "to argue for one's humanity, to angle toward freedom from various forms of social and cultural bondage and hegemony, and to challenge all forms of oppression."[3] This was education born of theft and fugitivity, as slaves (often under threat of death) and indigenous peoples taught themselves how to read the scripts of the European masters. They entered the language, thought forms, and cultural sensibilities of their colonizers and masters, aware but not fully aware of the price that would be paid to build freedom from the master's tools of bondage.[4]

Each generation of former slave and indigene saw, in thankfulness and criticism, both their predecessors' accomplishments in and their captivities to a house of educational bondage. This has been not only a history of progress and struggle but also a history of assimilation. Like master formation, this emancipatory formation also hides as it assimilates, sending up the message that it is engaged in a moral formation that cultivates people into advocates for justice and discerning citizen subjects able to spy out the signs of oppression.[5]

These two ways of educating born of the master's house have never been mutually exclusive. Both education as master formation and education as emancipatory weapon aim at cultivating mastery—the freedom of mastery (moral formation) or the mastery of freedom (emancipation)—and both silence the sound of a door opening to a life together, toward a formation in communion. Of course, this tragedy formed in the master's house.[6]

. . .

I remember my worst student and my worst time as a teacher. Connor was a middle-aged white guy from deep in the South, born and raised in the hateful power that structured an abiding racial antagonism. Connor carried that structure in his soul. But Connor also carried a deep love for his faith and a great respect for black preachers and ministry. He was the son of a minister, aiming to be a minister himself. He was the contradiction that one often meets in America and especially in the South—middle-aged white people who love much in black culture but are at war with black people. Connor had even attended and graduated from an HBCU (historically black college or university), because he could go as "a minority" and get significant tuition support. He and I met in my course on the history and theology of the black church, and we never knew a moment of peace together in that course. Connor believed he knew as much or more than I did about African American history, black church life, the plight of black people, and what needed to be done for us. He refused to let me be his teacher and with eager energy pressed me during each class period to be his student.

Connor did know a lot about the matters of the course, more than all the other students, but he turned all that knowledge toward a pathological reading of black folks. Each class period he turned everything we read and everything we discussed toward a black lack—of stable family life, of moral formation, and of proper education. And each class period made more visible the truth I wanted to deny: that I truly hated Connor. My faith in teaching, in Christianity, and in the academy was crumbling in this course as I felt helpless against my hate. Indeed, I cherished my hate.

The wall between anger and hate broke, and I was floating in the water until I could no longer feel the ground under my feet. How do you restore a wall when you cannot feel the ground? You release the anger until the waters of hate recede and you feel the ground again. Then you rebuild that wall.

But there was something else that I experienced with Connor— a woundedness and a longing. I could see that Connor's adversarial posture bothered him and that he wanted to be something more than a racial antagonist. He wanted to connect with me—to have me walk into his life, walk with him in his life. But he had no way to allow me in as a teacher and as cotraveler on the journey of faithfulness. Whiteness was embedded in his thinking like thick weeds in a garden, and I had neither the energy nor the interest to separate wheat from malignant chaff. For this I carried sorrow, because I knew Connor wanted to be a minister, but I could not help him: all I could do was resist him.

. . .

CHAPTER 4

Connor was a racist, but that was beside the point. We were caught in an educational motion or endeavor structured in antagonism, master formation versus emancipation. What the learning environment could be for me and for him carried the severe limitations to which we have all adjusted.

We sat together in our exhaustion, the black faculty members, eating lunch together, a few weeks left in the semester. Each of us on this day would be teaching our thorn class—the class with students who resisted our presence, challenged our authority, and made us work harder to prepare and teach than any faculty member should ever have to work. It was never a whole class, just the one or two, three or four students who reminded each of us that we lived in the master's house. As we finished lunch and conversation, I began to recite the words "Take my yoke upon you, and learn of me . . . ," and my colleagues finished them in unison, "for my yoke is easy, and my burden is light . . ." Then we all laughed out loud, probably in absurdity and hope. I whispered as we walked back to our offices, "and you will find rest for your souls."

Educational institutions assimilate. They draw people into a way of life by drawing people into sight of ways of life. Such assimilation can be thick or thin depending on how pronounced that way of life is in a curriculum or a social ecology, and in the way the layers of thinking, feeling, and acting move between students, faculty, and administrative staff. This is their glory. Colonialist educational assimilation turned education into an imperialist endeavor, forcing a way of life that would reduce ways of life. Colonialist assimilation draws people down to silent objects even when they speak. They become anticipations of an echo, with variations, but nonetheless an echo. This is an assimilation that hides itself as assimilation. It can be hidden in such practices as critical thinking, or traditioned reflection, or the repetition that makes for skilled execution of a task, gesture, or performance. This is our curse. Echoing in and of itself is not the problem. All education rightly carries an element of the echoing back. The problem here is the absence of a reciprocity of echoing that speaks of life aimed at the together.

. . .

I remember the painful discussion I had at a college committed to educating its new reality of diverse students. The demographic shift at this school was dramatic, with significant increases of African American, Latinx, and central and east African students. Most of these students were the first generation in their families to attend college. Some of them sat in on this discussion with faculty and administrators and me. I dreamed with the group of a reverse assimilation. A few of the faculty members quickly ended that dream. "There is nothing a nineteen-year-old student can teach me," said the senior professor of philosophy and theology. Almost thirty years of teaching students how to think critically, how to read texts and write clearly, had given him a clarity on his task that was truly impressive, but that clarity did not extend to his own life and the lives of his students. He went on, "I can see how knowing more about my students' background, their struggles, and so forth may help me in the task of teaching them, but it is not going to alter in any significant way what I do and have always done." Another professor spoke now, building on what his colleague said. "My goal is to help prepare these students to face a world filled with injustice and to expand the vision of the world they bring when they come to this institution." This second professor was a historian who specialized in twentieth-century religious and social movements with a special focus on Malcolm X. The irony of his statement escaped him. I looked in the eyes of the students present. Some looked down, others looked away from the circled chairs, but most looked into my eyes registering a silence that was far more than their absent voices.

.   ·   .

❧

I felt the old anger. It had returned. But now the wall was built back again and I could keep the anger from flooding my soul, filling me with hate, and pulling me off my feet, taking from me a sense of the ground. God had done this for me.

❧

These seasoned professors misunderstood my invitation to assimilate as meaning learning more things about their new students, coming to know their worlds, and aligning that knowledge with their knowledge. In such a frame of thinking and knowing, education is a calculation of exchange. How much do I need to know in order to give the student what I know? But if assimilation means lifeworlds brought inside lifeworlds, then something historically urgent and spiritually crucial is at stake in this moment. I was after something else with them—a deeper reality of entanglement. An entanglement in which they might give up attaining mastery, or possession, or control, and turn their entire school toward deeper involvement with the lifeworlds of their students whose communities surrounded and extended beyond the institution. To reverse that assimilation through the cultivation of an institutional reality of communion requires a new sense of shared habitation—geographic, intellectual, spiritual—and a new goal of self-articulation, to hear the many speaking through the one. Behind those students were communities that were a call to those professors to rethink their lives in their expansion in and toward both their students and those communities. But in order to hear that call, we who inhabit institutions need to know how to move back and forth from inside to outside.

Motions

❧

The phenomenological teacher

Being never safe,
I always envied the phenomenological teacher
They could always stay in the air
above history
suspended between
Knowledge and belief
They could take
Peoples, ideas, hopes, dreams,
God, Jesus, the Spirit,
Islam, The Buddha, Mohammad, The Koran, the Bible,
Spiritualists, Pentecostals, Satanists
And present them all in the
3rd Person, singular or plural.
Being always skindarkbound and never the universal,
I could not get away with that
caught as I was in flesh and Spirit.
Phenomenologicals disappear
in teaching the "They"
the whiteness forming voice
from stage left aiming for stage right,
to be viewed by students
as knowledge itself for the taking
or leaving smooth and clean and in
pieces like a plate filled with different flavored options,
like a journalist in alluring drag,
handling them the same by not handling them
I, on the other hand, was only one option
Take it or leave it.

❧

We work in the inwardness, existing in the journey of the quiet, moving from inside to outside and back inside again. There are two elements that are crucial to an academic ecology and to educational institutions, especially theological institutions: introversion and introspection. They have the same Latin root, *intro*, meaning "to the inside." The latter includes *specere*, "to look at," and the former includes *vertere*, "to turn." Introversion is the state of being in which one is constantly thoughtful about one's own existence, while introspection is the act of looking inwardly. One could imagine their relationship to be one of being and act, the being of introversion and the act of looking inwardly—introspection. Introversion organizes the external world through an ongoing internal calculus, and introspection is the energy and activity that give life to that organization. Academic institutions are structured inside both introversion and introspection, and in turn these institutions structure lives within an introspection and an introversion. Let's designate this work of introversion and introspection as the formation of inwardness. In this regard, academic institutions remain inside the ancient theological trajectory of contemplation.

Contemplation is everything in the history of Christian thought. We were formed to contemplate God. It is at the beginning of our journey, and it will be at the end of it as we enter into the eternal reality of contemplating the divine life. From the magnificent root of Christian contemplative practice grew the fundamental structures of Western education and especially theological education. Even educational institutions that imagine themselves far removed from these contemplative roots, having exorcised the religious and the theological from the way they imagine their intellectual work, are yet on the terrain of a theologically drenched vision of reflection, solitude, and self-examination. The monastic gesture is yet performed in the modern educational setting.

Introversion and introspection, however, are troubled in the master's house, penetrated by a calculus that mangles our inwardness and that often turns our thinking torturously insular, making the possibility of deep, abiding communion seem like an impossible dream.

. . .

I remember Rachel and Louise, these women both of a Philadelphia. Louise, white, from Philadelphia, Pennsylvania, and Rachel, black, from Philadelphia, Mississippi. Their friendship began in promise and ended in pain. They—both courageous and thoughtful—were willing to work at a friendship. But that work was clouded, as each was a layered thinker, analyzing and dissecting her actions and words toward the other. The chaplain and the dean of students and I were exhausted just watching them working at their relationship and thinking their relationship. Rachel thought her blackness, Louise her whiteness, Louise thought Rachel's blackness, Rachel thought Louise's whiteness, entering and exiting shadow and light as they corrected and explained, apologized and asserted their separate beings. They fought with the real and the imagined in their relationship and finally, as they approached the final semester of their program, Rachel said she had had enough—the friendship was over. What occasioned this break was less a thing between them and more one more racial event in the news, another senseless police-initiated shooting, more black mourning, and then the stupidity of whiteness explaining away the horror and the offense of another black death.

Louise was truly heartbroken, her tears heavy and constant in my office, and in the chaplain's office, and in the dean of student life's office. She could not bring her mind to a rest as she searched for the site of failure in herself. Rachel mourned as well. Her tears were reserved only for me and other black spaces. She searched as well for why she ended a friendship that yet carried promise and pleasure that neither she nor Louise was ready to admit. Rachel wove comments, words, ideas that Louise uttered over their several semesters together with the painful white explanations for black death and found Louise somehow closer to those from whom Rachel wanted great distance. The result: Louise gone.

. . .

Rachel was not wrong and Louise was not innocent. Louise was not wrong and Rachel was not innocent. They were working and thinking, and that was right and good and holy, but their working and thinking carried a torture that we could not articulate. They could see the work that needed to be done to be together, but they could not see that they were together, beholding one another's journeys and holding one another in thought and hope.

The pain present was not the overthinking of their relationship but the thorny trail of moving from inside to outside, from their own individual thoughts to their conversations and back to their thoughts and then to the expectations that surrounded them—of mastering the racial problematic in their own lives—and back to their thoughts, then to their relating, and back to their thoughts.

Rachel and Louise were caught in what we in the academy are all caught in—an introspection and an introversion permeated by the aspiration for self-sufficiency. But the drive toward self-sufficiency when joined to the realities of reflection, solitude, and self-examination creates a cruelty, like a biting dog that cannot be trained. The cruelty for Rachel and Louise showed itself precisely in the evaluative habit of mind that moved between them. Louise was not Connor—someone trapped in racial antagonism. She thoughtfully worked at unraveling the racial fabrics that covered her life. Rachel was willing to imagine a different state of being with her white friend—one in which she trusted the new. But in a space that demands self-sufficiency and aims at its displays, no one is able to stand, or more exactly, only one is able to stand—the one who achieves the image of a man finished.

The finished man was always the image held up and held out to colonized peoples in the processes of Western education. *The first work of that image is to create inadequacies.* This is the energy inside the master/slave dialectic within the legacies of plantation and colonial education. The first word of self-justification that masters told themselves was that the slaves had deficiencies that needed to be addressed. Slavery and colonialism always carried a therapeutic wish bound up in a soteriological illusion: they were addressing the deficiencies of the natives. For hundreds of years, generations of indigenous scholars and colonialized subjects have written powerfully and eloquently about the creation of the image and the inadequacies.[7] Everyone must aim toward the finished man, toward a self-sufficiency that overcomes their inadequacies.

. . .

I remember when Stonewall quit. That was his nickname. We were doctoral students at the same time. He in a school on the West Coast of the United States, and I in an East Coast program. We were together at a gathering for doctoral students of color seeking additional financial support to make it through our programs. We had both passed our preliminary examinations (qualifying examinations in other contexts) and were deep into drafting our dissertation proposals. This gathering included established scholars of color and white scholars who were allies. This was not an enjoyable time. We were mercilessly questioned about our ideas, our proposals, and our vocation. At breakfast on the last day, Stonewall and I were sitting at a table with an African American scholar and one of his African American doctoral students who had successfully defended his dissertation and now had a tenure-track job. After a few pleasantries, they both started in on Stonewall in a continuation of their grilling of him from the previous day. They told him that he needed to read more widely beyond what he had already read and that he needed to master his German and he needed to attend to his French more rigorously and what about Latin given his interest and be careful of the limitations of his dissertation director whose thinking was too narrow. . . . The light was gone from Stonewall's eyes. All he said in response was "This is what I get there. I thought it would be different here." I did too. Stonewall left the meeting and left his doctoral program—too many inadequacies.

. . .

The inwardness of the academy is a troubled inwardness that brings a form of diseased evaluation. This diseased evaluation was formed through the longitudinal effects of years of inside assessments always tied to a white male persona, standing at every evaluative juncture of an academic life and a professorial career. The problem is not that judgments are made but that they are spoiled. They arrive to us already old and stale, filled with the colonialist's tormenting spirits that are unleashed on us and that we then unleash on each other, moving from institution to institution, always turning judgments both local and contingent into a contorted universal perspective on people and their work. Here the white gatekeeper moves inside psychic space haunting interpretations of work and professional life and interrupting genuine self-affirmation. I have known too many scholars who have fallen into an abyss of critique or concealment against critique, moving through the academy in constant shadowboxing, throwing punches at anyone and everyone, bobbing and weaving, bracing for the impact of words that will surely sting. So many in response form a spirituality of resistance to that gatekeeper, but the point is that an unwanted glaring light has invaded the good work of introspection and interrogation. That glaring light slowly draws introspection and interrogation toward a form of surveillance that aims at control.

> Search me, God, and know my heart,
> Probe me and know my mind.
> And see if a vexing way be in me,
> And lead me on the eternal way.
>
> — Psalm 139:23–24
> (Robert Alter translation)

There is a joy in not knowing. Like a ribbon of a bow being opened to a gift, the not-knowing opens curiosity and curiosity enters wonder, as Lisa Sideris suggests. This is wonder that hosts knowledge, allowing it to grow within the beauty of mystery.[8] Not knowing is glorious energy that fuels intellectual life, pressing us to listen and learn, drawing out both an impatience and a patience that work collaboratively. But what happens when the not-knowing is turned into a weakness, like a hole in one's armor or a flaw in one's fighting technique? What becomes of the not-knowing when it becomes a crime and calls forth punishment? In the colonial master's house, the not-knowing became a burden for inwardness, and a burdened inwardness. Colonial subjects were instructed to accept a searching and a probing that would locate the not-knowing and eradicate it, like a virus. Of course, what was not known was the world of the European in its fullness—its languages, its logics, the proper expressions of its cultures, its knowledges, and its ways of forming and framing knowledge. Such a not-knowing was endless, so the searching would be endless.

My voice trembles
always at the sound
of your voice, which began
for me so long ago, gently
guiding me to what was
good, great, weak, strong,
straight into the vise,
tightening ever so slowly
that I mistake the hurting
for stability, constrictions
for conscientiousness. I learn
labored breathing, tighter
    thinking
until I make the sound for help
with every sound I make. But I
think, this will not be forever.
I will break free even if I must
tear skin from my flesh to
loose your stability.

Sara saved her, took Joan
from the other voice
and placed her inside.
She knew how, having lost
enough skin to form a womb
outside her body—the
    mindbodywomb—
where bathing light would cover
Joan's thinking, protecting her
from glaring light—light against
light knitting truth into
her inward being before it
could be snatched away by
the other voice, until she emerged
from Sara's wombbodymind
    intact,
and hearing none, the i passed
unharmed into Joan's voice
    flowing
like refreshing waters ready to
heal torn skin and cracked voices.

Many have rebelled against that search by pushing back against an academic institutional pathology that constantly tries to weave the good of not knowing into the horror of colonially formed inadequacies. Students, however, have a more difficult time discerning the difference. Some come to our institutions having had teachers who banished that shadow over their learning by celebrating the goodness of not knowing. They reduced Europeans from masters to learners and placed them alongside their students as colearners. Other teachers, however, pressed their students into full search mode, looking for their weaknesses, working feverishly to make their students into the finished man.

The lie is that in order to know the world, one must know the European world. The truth is that in order to know the world that has come to be, one must know the European world. The calamity is that coming to know the world should never have been put in this way. Students come to us confused about the search for knowledge, trying to find that difference between the honor of not knowing and the shame of colonial inadequacy, or they come to us in acute collapse, having merged the search to become the finished man with the search to know and understand.

The question is not what they should know. Too many educational institutions are lost in that question, looking obsessively at the commodities of learning. The question is, what should be the shape of the journey to know? What should be the character of the search? How might there be a shared inwardness that opens the joy of not knowing inside the joy of learning together? Yet here we must return to the rough ground of colonialism's forced intimacy.

Slaves had no choice. They were inside what they did not want to be inside of—the masters' and mistresses' longings, desires, and fantasies all played out in front of them and oftentimes on their bodies. Masters and mistresses

believed they had a right to the inner life of the slaves, because that was also their property. Slaves did, however, have a choice about what they allowed inside them—if not in their bodies, certainly in their minds and hearts. Masters and mistresses could pry open cracked doors in weakened bodies, yet even with forced entry, what they often discovered was not a slave's inner life but just another room without a view. But the right to know lingers long after slavery's end as well as the stubborn desire to center an intimacy born of whiteness where the search to know and understand remains plantation-like—with people of color made enhancers of knowledge, tools for use.

✦

. . .

I remember those weary minds. I was speaking at a Christian college in the aftermath of a few racial incidents on campus that were evidence of the resurgence of white supremacy's confidence. The students of color were feeling the stress of it all. I looked in their eyes and I saw the truth I knew too well, having gone to a college just like theirs—very Christian and painfully white—and I spoke a truth that all needed to hear. I said that students of color carry a double burden in their schools. In one arm they carry the weight of racial harm, of aggressions small and large, and in their other arm they carry the fatigue of their friends. Eyes opened wide as I spoke. They attend their classes, I said, hoping to learn just like other students learn, only to hear all too often an ignorance laced in the knowledge of their professors, an ignorance of them and of the racial world they all shared. And then they return to the private spaces of dorm rooms and meal halls and study rooms and places off campus, only to find they have a new job—teaching and explaining, debating and exposing the racial truths that they are only beginning to deeply understand themselves. Their friendships with white students and some assimilated students of color carry a labor totally unfair and cruelly taxing. This is why, I said, so many students of color by the time they are seniors are sick of their schools and sick in their schools. The joy of not knowing was taken from them in the work of having to know, and the joy of their friendships died in the heat of an exhaustion that they feel but cannot explain. At that moment, many students of color stood up and cheered; others sat crying—water in a thirsty land.

. · .

Many students of color arrive at our institutions friendship-fatigued and rightly suspicious of an educational journey that promises more burden. They yet aim for friendship, but they are skeptical of the depth it can reach, not because of time or space but because of a habit of mind born of the plantation that centers the feelings and needs of white bodies and turns such students of color into service providers in a search of shared knowledge. At the same time, they are entering an academic ecology that is itself suspended between isolation and exhaustion—the exhaustion of striving toward the finished man and the isolation of a cruel, constant self-examination.

Under these conditions, self-examination and interrogation feed a kind of segregationist sentiment and mentality that is a creeping malady plaguing our institutions, creating in us an isolationism that weaves together an individualism bound to an exploitative disposition. It teaches us to ask the question, "What can I get out of this place or this person?" I am not referring to the formation of affinity group meetings, or the processes of self-selection that go into course choice, or disciplinary interests, or curricular design, none of which should be singled out as problematic because such endeavors and gatherings are generally efforts to overcome the long histories of exclusion. The point here reaches to the work of institutions in creating the conditions for a productive inwardness, one in which introspection and introversion are life giving and communion gesturing.

MOTIONS

Ash

He could not see my ashes,
it being Wednesday and me
being so dark.
No need to see, he laughed.
Forty again, no mule this time
as I traveled inward
looking to remember
but finding ashy
legs, ankles, arms, hands
shamefully present without
oil and dirt in my mouth
bent down as I was with
Ashé

his torture, each step hounded
Ashé
by their ignorant laughter,
inappropriate after Tuesday so far from
Sunday morning, moving forward is
labor too tight for sweat, but this is what
I want to be ash of shared pain and suffering
denying nothing, absolutely present
when the ash becomes dust
and takes on immortality,
then I will breathe again
and laugh,
Ashé

We must come to revolution. The word has no natural confluence
with education, the former an overturning and the latter a build-

ing up. In the history of Western education, revolution has been an object of study far more than a goal of formation. Indeed, the education born of the plantation and colonialism lives in the aftermath of revolution—the overturning of native worlds for the sake of establishing a new one. The new world that has come into existence formed educational institutions inside the refusal of revolution—one cannot have an overturning of an overturning, especially if the former overturning is understood to have established the common good, regardless of the screams and cries of native millions. Educational institutions can, however, entertain revolution as an idea worth exploring, mapping, even projecting as a possibility but always within an established way of being that intimates a resistance to change.

But the idea of revolution confronts theological educational institutions with a question: Why do you exist? This is our question because we exist inside a revolution, the overturning that is the turning the world right side up by God. It is an overturning that makes possible a beautifully strange kind of building up. It is a building up inside a crumbling. We are inside the Spirit's crumbling of world orders, orders that reach all the way down to the body, claiming sovereignty over the ways we should understand ourselves. Yet we are an overturning that has been drawn into the colonial overturning, and our energies have been harnessed in establishing the plantation as a world order. And although we have formed our educational institutions inside that world order, we yet carry the contradictions.

We are an overturning that facilitates a building up, but it is a building up that glories in the crumbling. Contradiction. We are an overturning that has been co-opted by the long legacy of colonialist overturning that marshaled our considerable energies in sustaining systems of instruction and evaluation that yet signal the plantation world order. More contradiction. Theological education is caught in these contradictions. The first contradiction is good and right but difficult to grasp because through it we build in revolution, we build institution in the midst of an overturning and a passing away. The second contradiction is a tragedy. It hurts us because through it we build institution always against an overturning, always to maintain an order we have mistakenly come to believe is good for us and good for the world. Understanding how we come to this mistake is crucial to figuring out how we can together move in new directions, move in the revolution.

. . .

I remember when he took me to lunch, this man for the season. He was one of the most powerful people at the university, having served in several high-profile and important positions. Over many decades, he had amassed incomparable influence and had mentored many in the university and the divinity school. I was only a few years into teaching and only a few months into actually voicing my opinions in faculty meetings. I spoke of the need for diversity, for change in our pedagogies, and for more attention to be given to our students of color. Nothing very radical, just earnest. Even so, it was clear that some of my opinions were not being well received by some of the senior faculty. So he decided to take me to lunch for a gentle talk—just two colleagues sharing a meal. He was the quintessential southern gentleman who spoke quietly and slowly, each word demanding your full attention.

He was also a storyteller. This, of course, is a constitutive aspect of being a powerful southern gentleman. So, he told me stories. The stories were about his humble upbringing inside the scent and sound of poverty, and within small suffocating circles of thinking. He came from nothing. Then he told me stories about the various faculty members he had known over the years. Each of these faculty members was extraordinarily gifted—sheer inexplicable intellectual power married to quirkiness in many. He mentioned one man (they were all men in these stories) who had memorized the intricacies of Immanuel Kant's critiques at the age of fifteen and had carried on a running argument against Kant for decades. Then he slowly and with the beautiful precision of a storyteller turned these stories toward a single point. "Any school that would have a significant future must always aim to gather together as many extraordinary people as possible and make no excuses for those who are not. A university or any academic institution must always be guided by the gifted." Then he said to me, speaking with that southern cadence I knew so well, "Willie, I have always lived thankfully in the privilege of being among such extraordinary people, and I hope you will as well. As you continue here, it would be good for you to follow the lead of your senior colleagues."

. . .

We have to recall at this moment what we know of the self-sufficient man. He wields power responsibly, never apologizing for fully acting in his abilities. What is also true of the self-sufficient man is that he identifies the sheer power of ability in others and never apologizes for identifying it. With this identification comes clarity about human beings and the way the world should be. Some are better than others—quicker, clearer, smarter, stronger, more gifted—and worlds, whether social, political, economic, or academic, should be ordered around such people. I am not sure if my would-be mentor imagined himself to be numbered among those with greater ability, but I am sure he did not imagine me in that number. He offered me this elitist anthropology as a kind of natural theology, that is, a way to recognize a divine intentionality for ordering the world through the natural occurrences of greater ability in some.

🌱

My parents had prepared me for him, this man of the old, because they were better storytellers than he was. I learned from my parents how to wield story with more precision than he did, how to use story as both shield and sword. Most importantly, I learned from them what story I was inside as I heard and told stories.

🌱

He showed me how educational institutions, especially theological institutions, often easily become imprecise defenders of the order of things. It happens in our ability to see ability. In the space between ability and seeing ability, a vision of order forms, moving from self-perception to a shared recognition of power. Academic institutions recognize three kinds of power: the power of intellectual ability, the power of notability (crudely designated as celebrity), and the power of money. There are other kinds of power, like the power to convene, but these three kinds of power shape sight. Scholars and administrators recognize power, and we sometimes see more than should be there. We see the way power makes things happen, and we commit *to the way* power makes things happen in and through powerful individuals. But the way to make things happen through those with power quickly slips from becoming a means to an end to becoming a stabilizing end in itself. We see an order to things that is in fact not an order but the imagined surest unit from which order must be built—the individual with power.

· · ·

I remember Winston, who went by the nickname Win. Every line for him had fallen in a pleasant place. His great-grandfather was a lumber baron, and his grandfather the governor of a state. Professors and Presbyterian ministers and businessmen dotted his family tree, and he had graduated from an excellent school in the Ivy Northeast. A tall, blond, blue-eyed, handsome, articulate young man who after two years of stellar work in divinity school at the start of his third year was being urged by my colleagues to go on to doctoral work. Win came to see me with a question. I will never forget his words: "I love my father and my grandfather and the other men in my life. I appreciate what they have given me. But I don't want to be them. How can I not be them?" I had waited all my teaching career for Win. He had been in my courses and those of my colleagues where a Being beyond the white self-sufficient man was beginning to be articulated, and Win heard what was being suggested. But now was the time of accounting for him and me as he was pressing me to help him see a way into that new being. I had no plan, only the sure knowledge that he would have to resist a world organized to build itself freshly on his body, making all things old through his newness. I also knew that once he left my office there would be very few people who would even understand his question.

. · .

Win was the first but not the last. Many have followed, and many such students inhabit our institutions trying to discern how to build a life inside a revolution that is being resisted and a crumbling that is being denied. Win knew how easy it would be for him to allow himself to become the building block of the old order, surrounded as he was by professors and family members who saw the perfecting of that order in him. Win needed friends who would discern with him the crumbling and live in it and toward it. He needed companions on a journey of building that together would discover what blueprints emerged from the overturning.

Do you hear the calling
from the new nothing,
not the old one
born of robbery and lack
but the nothing out of which
came that voice speaking light
to see clearly
the beginning of a new day
of rubble turned to hill and lifting head
and in an instant make refuse
the stuff of freeing legend
to glory thine be and belong

The shared work of discerning the overturning in the midst of the building is by far one of the most difficult tasks for theological institutions. That shared work is often confused or resisted. Theological schools tend to lean toward one of two types in relation to this difficult task:

Type A: Anxiety Academies

These are schools with students who are learning of their liberation and are seeking the revolution. The students want to embody it, and they want their institutions to embody it as well. So they practice this work—speaking truth to power, calling into question the social order, protesting policies, demanding that the old ways must fall—on faculty, staff, administrators, other students, trustees, and anyone who will listen to their activist voices aiming for victory. These students carry to varying degrees a righteous anger sometimes cultivated by the courses they have taken and the lessons they have learned from the school itself. But this is messy work, because motives are always mixed and clarity usually elusive. Clarity is elusive because we often collapse the overturning into thinking critically or engaging in political, social, ideological, or theological critique of the prevailing orders. We forget that critique itself is being overturned, turned right side up within the new purpose of life together. Critique must aim at communion. The overturning is wider and deeper than expressing the critical faculties. Administrators and faculty always make a terrible mistake when they forget that students must practice on us, learning to feel their righteous anger and express it appropriately. Students and faculty make a terrible mistake when they forget that communion is the point.

Type B: Silent Academies

These are schools that work diligently to control dissent. They do this not because they hate dissent, but because they understand the work of building to require that it be managed properly.

From the admissions process, through faculty hiring and institutional governance, to alumni relations and the work of the board of trustees, these schools seek a clarity of purpose that joins all involved in a shared project of building. Their students come because of that clarity, and their faculty are there because they share in it as well. Yet these schools—faculty, staff, administrators, and students—often forget that clarity deepens and grows new like a perennial plant that returns for another season with bright new colors and differently shaped branches and fruit. Theological schools live in the soil of the overturning, which means that my metaphor is inadequate, because a new is always emerging that is not just a variation on the old but a new reality that brings with it a crumbling of the old. What remains, what is the same, is God. Unfortunately, such schools have learned to see the overturning as what God is doing in the world but not in their schools.

❧

On the last day of worship
many souls yet present after finals
the summer already filling the sanctuary
we all wait for the service to begin
then we will hear in each other's voices once more
that sound that creates new worlds
soon we will depart with that hidden power.

❧

And then there is the money.

Money is already a story. Money has been an ever-present sign of commitment to a way of life. The New Testament designation of mammon captures this reality nicely. We are caught always between God and mammon, caught between the way God organizes relations and the way relations are organized by mammon. While we could easily slip into a Manichaean logic in talking about God and mammon, in truth we are inside both of their stories. The story of mammon is inside the story of God, and the story of God is inside the story of mammon. The incarnation formed this dilemma for us, becoming a crucial site of struggle. Jesus was subject to the power of mammon, and mammon was made subject to the power of God through Jesus. We live under mammon and we live under the reign of God. These are not equal statements, but they share a fierce urgency. That fierce urgency penetrates our work and life.

How will we live? This is the crucial question for theological institutions. By this question we are asking both how will we survive and what will be the character of our surviving. The double meaning of the question helps to locate the ways we lose sight of the overturning and the crumbling. Theological institutions are caught in the treacherous economic currents that are destroying so many in this world. Students come to us in the currents, feeling and knowing their pull. The students may or may not come to an institution that has enough resources to allow them a reprieve from hard swimming—from working long hours to make ends meet, from living hand to mouth or paycheck to paycheck and carrying ever-growing stress as they move through their theological education. Some students come resourced and are spared financial anxiety, but they too keep a keen eye on shifting currents, making sure they will not turn against them. But between the anxiety of an institution and the anxiety of students lies the real danger of alienation.

How did misery slip in?
Bound as we were
to promise and hope,
our hands all turned
out and up waiting for
the latter rain to touch
our dry lips and then we

sealed our tongues as we
looked for fruit from trees
closer to own, listening
to him tell us the differences
between us, no God here,
from there we struck out,
missing the reason for our hands
in the first place, their identical
being their identity for shared
feeding, filling, touching, holding
the water that will surely come
and wash away need but not
want that will be turned into
more hands

Alienation is distance where there should be none, and denial of the deep connection that is the birthright of living creatures and living prosperously as creatures together. The Western world is submerged in alienated labor, which means that the quest to make and get money often cultivates the severest segregation and deepest suspicions of people and institutions. A soul-crushing silence exists between institutional need and student need in many places where unrequited feelings pass like ships in the night, missing each other by inches and minutes. So many schools agonize over not having enough money to make the education and the school living free and easy and needing to take from students their hard-earned resources and more of their freedom lost in financial debt. So many students agonize over not having enough money to make the education and the school living easy and needing to find resources when sources are slim or costly. But the feelings almost never meet, barred as they are by shared doubt. Students will often doubt that the institution is doing all it can do to ease their burden. It finds money for some things, they suppose, but not enough for them. Some schools will doubt that their students are exercising enough frugality, discipline, sacrifice, and maturity in how they handle their money. The word often spoken by students and school alike for this situation is "entitlement," which is shorthand for "we are alienated from each other."

What do we share? This is the question that God demands we ask ourselves after we have asked the question of how we live. Sharing is the key that moves us from mammon to God. Even its gesture shakes the foundations of ways of relating built on dehumanizing processes of exchange. The overturning begins in the sharing and the sharing opens to eternity. Sharing crumbles a world of possession, exchange, and debt formed through mammon's way of organizing living. This is the trajectory that theological institutions are on: we share what we have and we cultivate an education in sharing. We share in hope that we will come to see each other at the journey's end even as we journey together toward God.

. . .

I remember consulting with a school that wanted to form a teacher-training program for its doctoral students who, as a group, were in very bad financial shape. The school provided very little monetary support, charging the students half tuition and paying them little for loads of teaching. There was plenty of discouragement and resentment to go around and few ideas of how to get out of this terrible trap. I asked the faculty and administration if they could make a simple gesture. The doctoral students commuted to school and squeezed meals into their backbreaking schedules, so I asked if the school could provide one of their on-campus apartments reserved for visiting guest speakers as a lounge and napping area for them, keep food in the refrigerator for them, and as a faculty and staff provide free meals three times a day for them. The school was strapped for cash, but there was unused gospel lying all around.

. . .

I have again covered a lot in a chapter, aiming at an urgent institutional need: to change our operations, that is, to change our motions in the spiraling wind, terrifying as that may feel to some, given the utter uncontrollability of it. But this is an inescapable place—nothing hides from wind—that never stands still but that calls us to the vulnerability of motion itself where balance is fragile, direction constantly needed, and falling down is a real possibility. But so too is a reality of formation that presents an assimilation, an inwardness, and a revolution that help to form an erotic soul, much like Mary's son who came to gather us. Yet it is precisely the problem of gathering that I need to consider as I end this brief meditation on formation. We already live in the midst of a process of gathering, a global gathering that does not cultivate life but pulls us toward a bondage and death found in a managed diversity and a stupefying docility. This is not the crowd but the crowd in chains, and only holy desire that forms in us for one another can break those chains and guide us to a place where we meet each other in ways that announce eternity.

5

Eros

Desire. A God secretly intoxicated
by dirt and water, breathing it
in and out.

Now, Mary thinks,
desire will say more to them
than death, and they will know
a way forward.

We were not the first to gather people. Christians were latecomers to a process that has always existed—a process of gathering people. Ancient powers, whether pharaohs or caliphs, shamans or princes, soldiers or priests, prophets or merchants, always gathered people together, seeking to verify or solidify their power, convey their dreams, or bring order to their worlds. There is nothing inherently good about gathering people together, but there is something inherently powerful.

Greed has always haunted gathering.

Some people hoard and some people have been hoarded. Both realities of hoarding meet us in the history of modern colonialism. From the slave ship to the hacienda, from the plantation to the field, from the mine to the market, people were gathered as a means to an end: to marshal their collective energy for mass work—planting, harvesting, clearing, building, capturing, loading, unloading, and of course fighting, especially to seize indigenous lands.

Those Christian colonialists moving back and forth between old and new worlds and between the conquest sites of the new worlds saw what few people had ever seen before—a vast array of peoples spanning heretofore incomprehensible distances, differences, and ways of living. In response to that sight and in light of their unquestioned power in those new places, these colonialists organized peoples in thought and space, and set in place a way to gather people that we are yet to escape, and maybe can never escape. Race, religion, and nation formed in that gathering work, each itself an unwanted conceptual gathering crafted in the power of whiteness. These forms of designation were unwanted because they were unnecessary for peoples who knew who they were in relation to the land, to animals, and to their gods, and how they were in relation to other peoples.[1] But race, religion, and nation became useful designations for theft, inside the work of separating peoples from the land.

People groups have always existed, but it was not until the modern colonial moment that those peoples were forced to think themselves in the troubled togetherness of race, religion, and nation in a world being stolen, privatized, segmented, segregated, commoditized, and bordered. We inherited troubles. The troubles were not the differences in peoples, in their different ways of being in the world, in believing in the gods or not believing, in acting, or in thinking, or even in negotiating with or struggling within those differences. These were and yet are the challenges that come with being creatures. The troubles are something else. The troubles are found in how we have come to think and know our differences through the operations of a thick whiteness. The world nurtured by Western colonialism is a world living in the tormenting innovation of thinking ourselves and thinking our differences as racial, religious or nonreligious, and nationalist beings.

We live in a defeated conceptual moment when so many have

surrendered their imaginations to working inside the ideas of race, religion, and nation as the most rational way to think collective existence and for peoples to know and announce themselves. It may be impossible to escape these ideas for thinking collective existence given how they are embedded in the world order formed through modern colonialism and enacted through education, but the more urgent question is whether we should continue to surrender our imaginations to them. The heart of the problem for us is not only that we are forced to think each other through these concepts, both individually and collectively. The heart of our troubles is also the way these concepts prepare us for a gathering governed by whiteness and the protocols aimed at its performance of control, possession, and mastery.

Whiteness invites us to imagine that we become visible to ourselves and others only through its narration of our lives. This was, however, much more than a thought exercise gone terribly wrong. It was inherent to the way Europeans transformed the world into private property and reorganized intellectual life within their cognitive empire.[2] They imagined they could see the peoples of the world better than the peoples of the world could see themselves, and that their insight was key to forming institutionalizing processes that were crucial to global well-being. They were as indispensable as God. Western education and modern theological education were formed in this condition without entering into lament over its harmful effects; indeed, we became the means through which untold generations were shaped to think inside these troubled forms of gathering and the facilitating obsession of whiteness with its relentless need to perform its indispensability.

• • •

I remember those wonderful students who looked at me with deep frustration. We were sitting at a large round table in a theological school in Canada. These were students from many places—First Nation students and students from various Caribbean islands, students from Ghana and Kenya and South Africa and South India, students from Korea and China and Vietnam, and even a couple of students from the United States. We had spent the morning together sharing beautiful stories of faith journeys that wove in and out of many faiths. Many journeys now moved in a hard-won Christian direction, others moved around Christianity, like birds circling an unsure tree, while others moved in paths not near Christian faith. All of these students worked with, lived with, and loved peoples of many faiths. These students loved their families and their communities of origin, and each student sought a way to honor those many faiths and those loves, even as they sought together to articulate their own faith.

It was the afternoon session that brought out the frustration, as we were then joined by Linda, a faculty member of the school, along with the academic dean, both white Canadians. Linda was talking about the matters that occasioned my consulting visit—curriculum development, interreligious engagement, and race. As she spoke, she explained the world—defining what religion and culture meant, suggesting what ought to be the contributions that religions and cultures make to each other and to the wider society, and charting the way for religions to achieve Enlightenment virtues. Some of what she said made sense, but all of the way she said it frustrated the students and me. They heard the same old plotting of their peoples and their lives on a journey not of their own choosing, but one pressed on them through the history of colonial relations and formations. That history arranged peoples on a line from ignorance to knowledge, from superstition to truth, from barbarity to civilization, and presented all peoples with limited options for imagining a journey together with others. The students, however, were working different journeys, trying to find a togetherness with their peoples and with each other. Linda, on the other hand, presented herself not on a journey but as a destination.

. . .

I am sure that Linda never imagined herself as a destination, but she had been formed and then positioned that way. The Western academy and the theological academy exist within the long history of colonial convening, forming a shared practice of speaking to and for the rest of the world.[3]

What would it mean to be a professor who thinks the gathering differently in a school that thinks it differently? It would first require we learn the difference between colonial gathering and a gathering that aims in a different direction, that is, a gathering that recalibrates journeys and turns us away from the limited colonial options for knowing and living with each other. Such knowing of the difference begins by understanding how people are formed into the facilitating obsession of whiteness.

This is a tale of two. Jane was born in quiet Colorado, grew up in an all-white suburb, went to an all-white school (except for the handpicked colorful few kids who were there for her to practice multiculture, a proxy for the world). She then went to a fine small liberal arts college, then to an evangelical school to get a master's degree, and then on to do a doctoral degree at a school of great reputation. While she was in all those schools she weaved her way through to the best faculty members (to her mind), avoided faculty of color except on social occasions, and was always very polite but never their student. She graduated, moved into an all-white community (except for the handpicked colorful few people who were there for her to continue practicing multiculture, a proxy for the world). She got a teaching job at a school, where she met Jack.

Jack was born in quiet Connecticut, grew up in an all-white suburb, went to an all-white school (except for the handpicked colorful few kids who were there for him to practice multiculture, a proxy for the world). He then went to a fine, fairly large liberal arts college, then to a self-acknowledged liberal-progressive school to get a master's degree, and then on to do a doctoral degree at another school of great reputation. While he was in all those schools he weaved his way through to the best faculty members (to his mind), avoided faculty of color except on social occasions, and was always very polite but never their student. He graduated, moved into an all-white community (except for the handpicked colorful few people who were there for him to continue practicing multiculture, a proxy for the world). He got a teaching job and was there to welcome Jane.

Jane and Jack became good teachers—thoughtful, considerate, and careful—but each was a Minotaur who lived in a labyrinth created for them and by them where all the paths of their students would always lead back to them. The journeys of their students dissolved in their labyrinths, becoming marks and carvings on their corridors. Jane and Jack each formed their world not through narcissism or ignorance, but through something worse, a carefully orchestrated self-formation that they imagined was finished and now served as the home to which the students were invited to aim and enter.

Their homes, however, could not actually accommodate the students. They sensed this, and they heard the quiet complaints of students, always around the edges of the real problem. I wanted to end their worlds and take down their labyrinths, but I was so very late, having never been to their corners of Colorado or Connecticut. Yet what truly thwarted my efforts was their impenetrable helplessness, their shared illusion that this was the way they were—their permanent composition. I had no time machine to take them back and show them they had been schooled in a sickness—had learned a distorted way of gathering inside a distorted way of thinking, a distorted way of thinking inside a distorted way of gathering.

The academy convenes. It draws people together, and facilitation is its birthright. This connotes a beautiful kind of centeredness where teacher and institution are gladly surrounded by the matters of life—of people, of problems, of questions, of theories, and of many things in between. The problem we face is a diseased centeredness, one sickened with something akin to a virus that begins to work in a body, moving from parts to the whole outlook of a person. This centeredness sickened by whiteness grew from the pedagogical imperialism of the Euro-colonialists who imagined the whole world as their students, expanded as their reformatting of the world expanded, took definitive shape as they formed educational projects across the planet, networked through their imperial languages and the formation, production, and dissemination of ideas and materials from books to maps, from classrooms to rituals of evaluation.

The facilitating obsession of whiteness performs less a consistent set of characteristics and more a consistent refusal—a refusal to envision shared facilitation, a refusal to place oneself in the journey of others, a refusal of the vulnerability of a centeredness from below (rather than from the towering heights of whiteness), where the sense of my own formation is not only still open, but where I am willingly being changed not by a nondescript other but by nonwhite peoples historically imagined at the sharp point of instruction. In short, this is a refusal to release oneself to the crowd.

Judgment

You can get away with that here,
They said,
the judgment was already rendered.
Your Being is Primate.
We, however, are Bypass.
You can pray to your gods in public,
They said,
You being Primate.
We, however, bypassed.
You can say "Amen," and scream, shout
out many words aimed at every
direction, You native, Indi-ground,
po'bo' burned Primate.
We, however, are passed.
You can dance, slinging your body
around the space as if a holy ghost
holds you up,

CHAPTER 5

Your Being is always Primate.
We, however, passed
into the night, where no one
works like that any more
and in the stillness
we can hear and feel you move
but we cannot see you.
The judgment was already rendered.

The subtlety of colonial gathering is very important. It is one thing for people to be gathered in their differences. It is another thing entirely for people to be told how to know, think, and negotiate their differences, and still another thing entirely to have differences created in front of their eyes and told generation after generation to see themselves and others through these manufactured differences.[4] People disagree, peoples disagree, but in the long histories of Western colonial education, rarely if ever have people or peoples been allowed to name and voice those disagreements separate from the refereeing positioning of whiteness.

"I don't see a way out," he said to me.
"These problems cover me too thickly," he said to me.
"Tattooed into my skin," he said.
"Really?" I said.
"I will take them to my grave," he said.
Then I said, "That sounds reasonable to me,
Nicodemus."

Why do we gather? Everything hangs on our answer to this question. This question has to be asked freshly beyond the colonial imagination. Just as the Western academy convenes, so too does the theological academy convene. But our convening is always undomesticated, imbued with the realities of the crowd, driven by a God who reaches everywhere and particularly to those not seen by conventional ways of seeing. But that convening must be unleashed from controlling desire, which means our convening will always be dangerous.

It was the crowd that wanted Jesus crucified, but Jesus yet wanted the crowd. Western education and especially theological education have not been able to digest this truth. To be turned toward the crowd is to be turned toward those who need but who also hate, those who hope for life but are also susceptible to the wooing of death, to become its agents. Fear is a crowd failing, violence is a crowd addiction, and ignorance is a crowd's stubborn habit of collective mind. Jesus knew this and this knowledge anchored his life, but it did not guide his life. Jesus came for the crowd, just as God comes for the creature.

God comes, aiming for ecstasy in the body of the creature. This must never be denied. To deny this is to undermine the central purpose of theological education—to give witness to God's embrace of the creature and the desire of God to make embrace the vocation of creatures that have yielded to the Spirit. The urgent work calling us in theological education is to touch the divine reality of longing, to enter into its power and newness as the logic inside the work of gathering and inside the formation that should be at the heart of theological education. Yet there is another effect of whiteness that thwarts our work. Beside its obsession with facilitation with its diseased centeredness, there is also the reformation of relationality within exchange networks.

The colonial form of greed aimed to destroy a communal metaphysic grounded in sharing, mutual ownership, interpenetrating uses of goods and services; bartering, buying, selling, borrowing, and exchanging all woven in relationships extended over time, relationships that were themselves enveloped in stories that gave rationale and meaning to such activities. Such communalisms were not utopias, nor were they immutable, but they were powerful ways of thinking the one in the many and the many in the one.[5] But the goal of the colonialist—whether trader, explorer, missionary, merchant, or soldier—was to reduce the many to the one as a point of negotiation, management, conversion, and profit. The goal manifested in every colonial site was to move people slowly but clearly from any kind of group thinking about their wants and needs to thinking like an individual who could enter into exchange over goods and services guided by a rationality freed from communal obligation except at the level of volition. Such people would form connection through capital and perform a relationality woven first and foremost in utility and aiming at profit. Exchange networks need not be personal, need not be communal, need not be storied, need not suggest long-term obligation or relationship, need not even require names or identities. They only require items and money, that is, commodities.[6]

1698, in a port city on the west coast of Africa,
near what is now Ghana,
the following conversation took place:
African I: What's your name?
African II: You don't need to know my name.
The earth starts shaking.
African I: What are you selling?
African II: This ox.
African I: Where did it come from?
African II: You don't need to know that.
The birds start crying not singing.
African I: How much do you want for it?
African II: I want guns and alcohol.
African I: I have that.

Many plants and trees collapse to the ground.
African II: Let's do business.
Two hands touch in agreement.
The world feels ruin.

☙

Exchange networks, however, may create something personal, communal, storied, and obligatory that leans toward mutual recognition and relationship. Exchange networks can form friendships. Of course, in this schema, without the commodities there is no community and friendship is an option. But this is a strange kind of friendship, created *ex nihilo*, out of nothing, and governed by an individualism that makes sustaining and cultivating the friendship a singular endeavor built on the strength and desire of the one for the other one. This is the world the colonialists put in place, and we have imagined community through it, which means that we have never really imagined community. This is quintessentially the work of whiteness. Ironically, it was the communal hospitality of so many indigenous communities that made the work and world of the colonialist possible in the first place through the willingness of indigenes to share land and life, food and practices for living together.

• • •

I remember Ben and Leonia and my disappointment over what they could not hear. I was there at this retreat center with a group of professors discussing teaching and relationship building with students. The group had shared deeply about the struggles of connecting to students, working with multiple challenges both in the students and in ourselves, and about connecting with the communities of the students. Ben had been a solid participant over those days, offering his advice and techniques on engaging students, but by the last full day of discussion he had had enough. Ben said he felt that we all were losing perspective on what the "business of education" was about (his exact words). "I am not here to be the student's mother, father, brother, buddy, or therapist. I teach Bible. My goal is to make sure they understand how to read texts. They pay for a service and I deliver that service." Then he aimed his next comments directly at me. "I think it is unethical and a denial of the power relationship between me and my students to cross the boundary of the student-professor relation, especially as a white man. These students don't come to my school to become my friend, but to get the education they came for." Leonia, an African American woman, said she agreed with Ben. "I am not trying to become friends with these students, especially the ones that don't respect me. My goal in the classroom is to establish my authority in what is already a dangerous and contested space for me. It is not a space of friendship."

In the four days of conversation, I had talked about sensing communion and building toward that sensing but never once had I talked about friendship. I wanted the group to find a way to see a different structure of relationality beyond the strange kind of relationships we inhabit through exchange networks. That vision of relationship aims at control, not of the would-be friend but of the conditions within which the friendship would exist. This is friendship shaped in an isolation imagined as focus— one on one—but is in fact a tragic suspension of the sinews of our connection. This is friendship imagined as what constitutes community. It is a work accomplished through the decision of the individual to will connection and share knowledge. But such a way of envisioning friendship denies the already—the entanglements and the enmeshments—that constitutes the realities of life.[7] It is these realities that were attacked by modern colonialism and that are constantly refused by the exchange networks of modern capitalism.

I asked Ben and Leonia what the worship and chapel services of their schools meant to them. What was the significance of singing and worship with students, holding hands and praying with them, sharing the eucharistic meal with them, sitting with them for hours in their offices, connecting with them online and through emails, listening and counseling them, eating meals with them, writing recommendations for them, encouraging them to stick with the course, or the program, or the education itself? Ben answered quickly with one word, "Work." Leonia pondered these questions and then said to me, "I see what you are getting at. But this is not friendship." "No," I said. "It is something so much more."

.   .   .

I am not suggesting there is no such thing as proper boundaries between faculty and students. Nor am I trying to dismiss the integrity of friendship or the efforts required to sustain it. I am challenging the prevailing vision of its constitution in the Western world and all the places touched by the legacies of colonialism. That vision is like having a swimming pool in the ocean with perforated walls that one imagines holds separate water, when it does not. Friendship is a real thing where people open their living to one another, allowing the paths of life to crisscross in journeys imagined as in some sense shared. We need such friendships. But friendships form on a social fabric before they create a fabric, and it is that social fabric that deserves much more attention and reflection first for the ways it has been deformed—creating the illusion that we are only actually connected by choice—and second for the ways it may be remade, making possible a reality of intimacy, communication, reciprocity, and mutuality that builds from a deepening sense of connection.

There are, of course, many who shun such sensing, having been raised in or subjected to a cruel communalism where a community demanded too much, withheld too much, gave too little, or simply tried to destroy their life. Such communities were places from which to escape, never to return. I have encountered many in the academy who glory in the safety of the individual and who feel freed from soul-killing communal optics and obligations. It would be wrong to see such folks as only those who have fallen victim to the corrosive effects of modernity, having stripped away from themselves their own social skin. There are communities that no one should inhabit, and there are forms of communalism that destroy healthy habitation. But escape is an act that can become a practice that can become a habit that can form us into social patterns fully captured by the exchange networks of capitalism. The tragedy occurs here when a social habit becomes an intellectual habit that wars against the communal in educational institutions.

At the very beginning of this book I mentioned the idea of escape. It is a motivation for going into the academy and being in the academy that must never be underestimated, and unfortunately it has been underestimated in its role in forming the energy that thwarts a formation in communion. So many scholars in the academy escaped. They are here in relief and release from where they are from in so many ways—economically, socially, culturally, spiritually, intellectually, and sexually—and they have vowed never to return. It is a private vow that often has public effect, turning some scholars and the institutions they inhabit into citadels against any hint of a communal vision that suggests the places of their former confinement. I am not saying that most scholars have an antagonistic relation to their places of origin, nor am I naming in Freudian fashion some psychological condition that plagues scholars. Indeed, some scholars are not refugees or fugitives of any sort. They inhabit an academy nicely aligned with the worlds out of which they came. I am pointing to an often-tacit shunning of the communal that shuts down the imaginative capacities of a scholar or an academic community to envision an ecology of learning that aims toward it. Those who have escaped often only imagine social life on the run where friendships form with suspicious and vigilant volunteers, always ready to escape once more if they sense confinement approaching. The formation we need overcomes that kind of friendship formation, but more importantly it presses toward a different kind of communalism. It presses toward a gathering that breaks boundaries and crosses borders.

So Peter said to Cornelius, "You know that we Jews do not associate with you Gentiles. I should not be here in your home. But
God showed me that I cannot any longer call anyone profane or
unclean. Now tell me why I am here?" (Acts 10:28–29)

The crowd is itself a destination and not a means to an end.
The goal of cultivating those who can gather people centers theological education in its erotic power. A number of feminist scholars have written powerfully about erotic power in varied ways that
all give witness to a deep energy in the world, which for many is
registered in the bodies of women.[8] As Audre Lorde said, "Within
the celebration of the erotic in all our endeavors, my work becomes a conscious decision—a longed-for bed which I enter
gratefully and from which I rise up empowered."[9] It is this erotic
power that draws us toward one another. Erotic power is, as Rita
Nakashima Brock states, "the power of our primal interrelated-
ness,"[10] and it is this power that is feared, resisted, or exploited
by those committed to patriarchy and to social forms that use the
ideas of coupling and the family to control this power, channel-
ing it to be used by nation-states and corporations to shore up
their destructive communal visions.[11]

Erotic power has been drawn in our time into the trajecto-
ries of colonial control rooted in whiteness and made malignant
through the racial segregation that has shaped and continues to
shape so many individuals and communities. Desire rooted in
control is disordered desire that inevitably forms social prisons
that drain life. Too many well-meaning people who have been
formed in social spaces constituted in and by whiteness perform
that malignant power in the way they touch, hold, and envision
the social.

. . .

I remember Ushi's exhaustion. She was the only Asian woman
on a faculty of fifteen—nine other women, all white, three white
men, one African man, and one Latino man. I met Ushi deep

into her tiredness. She had been at this school for five invasive years. It is never easy being the first or only woman of color on a predominantly white faculty, but Ushi was not prepared for the strange intimacy she experienced at her school. Her female colleagues were kind and caring but assertively familiar. They touched her. They touched her constantly with their hands and their words; neither felt like caressing care, but control. They, however, listened to her ideas, positions, and arguments selectively, hearing the words that sounded like them and dismissing the words that reminded them of her difference.

The breaking point came after a particularly difficult faculty meeting in which she spoke a lot but was heard very little. It was at the social hour after the faculty meeting that she surrendered to her anger. She stood in a group of colleagues trying to reiterate her point and announce her thinking but getting the same nonresponse and paucity of respect. As this informal conversation continued, they began again with the touching— hands reaching for the back rub, other women leaning into her body as though her space was their space, as though her body was their pet's body. Ushi felt herself squeezing the wine glass until it started to shake in her hand. Then she yelled loudly, her voice filling every cubic inch of that large room, "Stop touching me, goddammit!" She put down her glass of white wine and left the white room.

My visit came a year later, in the aftermath. Ushi recounted this story at our breakfast, just me and her, and told me of her new life at the same institution. Now she was streamlined. She taught her classes, met with her advisees, did her committee work, and left the campus seconds after her work was done. No social events, no wine, no cheese, prayers, worship, talks, events, panel discussions: to all she said, "No, thank you." Ushi disappeared into the silence that was already made for her in the school where she had a voice that was rarely heard. She simply hid her body in that silence as well.

.   .   .

EROS

A good preacher dreams / bodies swaying in full tilt / wide open to the eager wind-emotion, pulsating. She sees hands flowing / together in a sheet of sound / layered broken piercing / many and different / all gathering into sensing / Spirit complete the moment / when all feel the knowing / and then death gives way to victory / in a living that moves through walls / of histories that refuse doors. Now with eyes made stubborn by hope / we see a crowd's new route into each other / flowing from need to want / this will be, they think, what she waited for, tipping over the horizon, desire revealed.

Caught in the powerful currents of a history that moves through us, we inhabit a social world constricted through whiteness that has left us with limited options for imagining how we might be with each other. That social world, to be clear, does not need the presence of peoples of European descent to be active, strong, and destructive. It only needs desire deformed by colonialist urges to control bodies, aimed toward their objectification and exploitation. The distorted erotic power that fuels that world must be freed from its captivity to whiteness and turned back toward its source in divine desire.

We can start again. The "again" being a gift from the God who raised Jesus from the dead. Theological education exists in the "again." This is education that has as its fundamental resource erotic power, and that power finds its home in the divine ecstasy in which God relentlessly gives Godself to us, joyfully opening the divine life as our habitation. As Wendy Farley says, "The power of Christ is erotic; it is divine yearning and zeal."[12] This is power we enter through participation. The crowd surrounding Jesus gathers in the desire of God. The crowd gathers, and this is already on the way to being good news. The crowd is not Christian, but the gathering is in Christ. I am not suggesting by this a sort of sanctified event planning or an anonymously Christian crowd. This crowd forming gives witness to one who has yielded his life to divine desire. Jesus gathers in God—divine desire permeating his life and work—and now in him we see what God wants: communion.

Formation in theological education at its best is a showing of this communion.

By reframing theological education and Western education more broadly through a formation within the erotic power of God to gather together, I am turning attention to the original trajectory of a God who has ended hostility and has drawn all of creation into a reconciliation that we do not control. God offers us an uncontrollable reconciliation, one that aims to re-create us, reforming us as those who enact gathering and who gesture communion with our very existence. We end hostility.

This, of course, is a dream, but it is God's dream.

Education formed in this dream is yet to emerge. Theological education is closer to this emergence, but we have blocked our own way to it by constantly erecting an image that captures our imaginations and drains our energies. Western education has offered us a distorted vision of what an educated person should look like, and we theological educators have accepted it. My entire adult life has been spent in and around educational institutions watching a formation that leaves its greatest treasure untapped, a treasure that would move us toward a true maturity that is a way of life together, a way that forms new life together.

Education is an endeavor deeply inside desire. This I have also learned through many years in the academy. We gesture desire in everything we do in educational space, all of it gesturing a willingness to yield one's life in mind and body even if that yielding is extremely tentative and episodic, all of it aiming at what we want to be and become. That wanting has been intercepted by the wanting of another—an old man that haunts us—redirecting our wanting toward his blinding light so that we will not see even as we are educating people to see.

EROS

He blessed it and broke open his dream, one part in each hand.
To those on his left and those on his right, he said the same thing
as he handed them his dream, "Eat this dream,
and it will kill the dream that kills."
Hands trembling, they wondered which of their dreams
would die and which would grow stronger.

Theological education is in the midst of an epic struggle. This is not a struggle to educate the masses or the elites of this world, nor is it a struggle to bring formal education to those who function without it. And it is not the struggle to survive as a financially viable endeavor. This is a struggle against this old man and the world he has created for us. If there is a nexus of most of the massive problems of the world, then the wanting of this old man is that nexus. There we find massive operations—economic, geographic, political, social, and intellectual—that point to one relentless goal: dominion.

A microcosm of that nexus is found in the academy, which means what happens in the halls of educational institutions, whether those halls are in physical or digital space, intertwines with the energies that are carrying forward the designs of the old man. The idea of the academy as an ivory tower removed from the world has always been a dangerous illusion that hides the work of forming people to enter willingly into the wanting of that old man. The old man's wanting is inseparable from the coming of the white self-sufficient man, an arrival that is always a becoming. But it is the dreaming of his arrival that allows the old man to press himself into our future imaginings. This is the true horror of seeking possession, control, and mastery as fundamental characteristics of being the finished man, resting in an educated state of self-sufficiency: it never comes, but you live your life always aiming at it, dreaming the old man's dreaming.

He dreams in the academy and through the academy, his eternality manifest in our bodies and for our own good. To struggle against him is to struggle against ourselves and our desires turned in dismal directions. Our desires can be turned in a new direction, and they must be if we want to end the quiet suffering and the acute resignation that flows through educational systems in the West and all the places that follow its pedagogies, all the places where people with the privilege of going to school also enter the problem of a troubled journey.

Theological education could mark a new path for Western education, one that builds a vision of education that cultivates the new belonging that this world longs to inhabit. But we cannot give witness to that newness if we imagine that our fundamental struggle is one of institutional survival, or the challenge of educational delivery systems, or the alignment of financial modeling with our desired outcomes, or the expansion of pedagogical models. All these matters are important, but they are not where the struggle meets us or from where the vision of our futures will come.

．． ．

My last year in seminary, I was invited with a small group of African American men and women to represent the school at an interreligious gathering of students training to be Protestant ministers, Catholic priests, Jewish rabbis, and Muslim clerics. We met at a mountain retreat in Southern California for four days and three nights. We talked and laughed together, sang and worshiped together, each in our own religious world yet sharing that world with all the rest of us. On the last day, as we were leaving, a few of us from each group kept talking and sharing stories in the parking lot. We did not want to leave that moment because we felt the thickness of its unique joy. Finally, with the sun descending and only our few cars in the parking lot, we knew it was time to depart. So the hugs began. Everyone hugged everyone else until only the sound of our words of good-bye held us together.

Even as our time drained away like water poured on the ground, we wanted to linger together on the mountain.

. • .

The mountain waits—this is the promise of theological education—as people cross the thresholds of our institutions to be prepared to face the struggles of faith and the struggles for faith in this world. They see the mountain. But the mountain is more than an endurance, or a journey marked by hardship and dedication. The mountain is a place where we can linger in a surprising desire for one another, where stories and hopes bound up in dreams might be shared and we have time—that precious gift—to learn more deeply of a God who dreams a mountain for us all to make a home together. It is the mountain that orients our work and heals our souls, because there on the mountain, according to the prophet Isaiah, a stream of people from every tribe and clan will finally reach our destiny in God, and the education we have anticipated with all our institutions and all our teaching and learning will finally begin.

For Further Thought: Beyond the End

At the end of a semester, or an academic year, or a book, you hope that exhaustion has joined exhilaration, and those to whom you have offered your thinking and dreaming will move forward making beautiful steps of their own. I want to encourage you to make beautiful steps of your own by talking with your colleagues—students, faculty, and administrators—and asking them what things might you all read together, what conversations might you have, and what commitments to dialogue ought you to make. I recommend this rather than send you away from this text with a list of recommended reading, not because I am against further reading. My endnotes included several books worth considering reading, but the most crucial step would be for you to imagine new conversations that open up a shared exploration into the desire for communion that is intended to vivify theological education.

To be involved in theological education is to long for eternity and the end of death. It is to seek the blessed state where our words start to do new work by first joining the chorus of the words of those who live forever in the Lord and who sound the healing and redeeming voice of the living God. Then our words will heal. Then our words will build up. Then our words will help form life together. Then our words will give witness to a destiny only visible through love. Talking together then is a practice aimed at eternity, and it matters more than we often realize for bringing our hope into focus. This finally is the goal of this book and the task I want to leave you with—to bring hope into focus.

Notes

Prologue

1. My argument in this book draws inspiration and insight from the groundbreaking text *God's Fierce Whimsy: Christian Feminism and Theological Education* (New York: Pilgrim, 1985), written by the famous Mud Flower Collective, who were Katie Geneva Cannon, Beverly W. Harrison, Carter Heyward, Ada María Isasi-Díaz, Bess B. Johnson, Mary D. Pellauer, and Nancy D. Richardson. This text marked an important moment in self-reflection for Western theological education. While it was criticized after its publication, it has never received the appropriate attention for the way it framed the problem of theological education. See Stina Busman Jost, *Walking with the Mud Flower Collective: God's Fierce Whimsy and Dialogic Theological Method* (Minneapolis: Fortress, 2014). Similar insight comes from the important work by Rebecca S. Chopp, *Saving Work: Feminist Practices of Theological Education* (Louisville: Westminster John Knox, 1995).

2. Lamin Sanneh, *Translating the Message: The Missionary Impact on Culture* (Maryknoll, NY: Orbis, 1990); Andrew Walls, *The Cross-Cultural Process in Christian History* (Maryknoll, NY: Orbis, 2002).

3. Willie James Jennings, "Can White People Be Saved? Reflections on the Relationship of Missions and Whiteness," in *Can "White" People Be Saved? Triangulating Race, Theology, and Mission* (Downers Grove, IL: IVP Academic, 2018), 27–42.

4. Pierre Bourdieu, *Pascalian Meditations* (Stanford, CA: Stanford University Press, 1997). Read especially chaps. 4–6.

5. Unless otherwise indicated, biblical quotations in this book come from the New Revised Standard Version.

Chapter 1

1. Poem adapted from the hymn *I Love to Tell the Story*, by Catherine Hankey.

2. Toni Morrison, *The Bluest Eye* (New York: Plume Books, 1993).

3. Susan Zantop, *Colonial Fantasies: Conquest, Family, and Nation in Precolonial Germany, 1770–1870* (Durham, NC: Duke University Press, 1997); Jonathan Sheehan, *The Enlightenment Bible: Translation, Scholarship, Culture* (Princeton: Princeton University Press, 2005); George Steinmetz, *The Devil's Handwriting: Precoloniality and the German Colonial State in Qingdao, Samoa, and Southwest Africa* (Chicago: University of Chicago Press, 2007).

4. Edward Schillebeeckx, "Secular Criticism of Christian Obedience and the Christian Reaction to That Criticism," in *Christian Obedience*, ed. Christian Duquoc and Casiano Floristán (Edinburgh: T&T Clark, 1980).

5. I am following the use of masculine language faithfully here because it is precisely in the imagined form of a man that this virtue is realized.

6. The common motto that white men cited in educating Native American children was "Kill the Indian, save the man." The history of American Indian residential schools always revealed the organizing principle: to form self-sufficient white men of their men, of their women, of their children—or kill them. Ward Churchill, *Kill the Indian, Save the Man: The Genocidal Impact of American Indian Residential Schools* (San Francisco: City Light Books, 2004); K. Tsianina Lomawaima, *They Called It Prairie Light: The Story of Chilocco Indian School* (Lincoln: University of Nebraska Press, 1994); Francis Paul Prucha, ed., *Americanizing the American Indians: Writings by the "Friends of the Indian," 1880–1900* (Lincoln: University of Nebraska Press, 1993).

7. See Alasdair MacIntyre, *After Virtue* (Notre Dame: University of Notre Dame Press, 2007); Alasdair MacIntyre, *Whose Justice? Which Rationality?* (Notre Dame: University of Notre Dame Press, 1989); C. Kavin Rowe, *One True Life: The Stoics and Early Christians as Rival Traditions* (New Haven: Yale University Press, 2016).

8. See Robert Bellah et al., *Habits of the Heart: Individualism and Commitment in American Life* (Berkeley: University of California Press, 1985); Brad S. Gregory, *The Unintended Reformation: How a Religious Revolution Secularized Society* (Cambridge, MA: Harvard University Press, 2012); Stanley Hauerwas, *In Good Company: The Church as Polis* (Notre Dame: University of Notre Dame Press, 1995).

Chapter 2

1. Nancy Lynne Westfield, ed., *Being Black, Teaching Black: Politics and Pedagogy in Religious Studies* (Nashville: Abingdon, 2008).

2. Arturo Escobar, *Designs for the Pluriverse: Radical Interdependence, Autonomy, and the Making of Worlds* (Durham, NC: Duke University Press, 2018), 4.

3. Simone Weil, "Reflections on the Right Use of School Studies with a View to the Love of God," in *Waiting for God* (New York: Harper Perennial, 2009), 57.

4. Olga Weigers, *In Search of the Truth: A History of Disputation Techniques from Antiquity to Early Modern Times* (Turnhout, Belgium: Brepols, 2014); Olga Weigers, *A Scholar's Paradise: Teaching and Debating in Medieval Paris* (Turnhout, Belgium: Brepols, 2015); Ulrich G. Leinsle, *Introduction to Scholastic Theology* (Washington, DC: Catholic University of America Press, 2010).

5. Serge Gruzinski, *The Mestizo Mind: The Intellectual Dynamics of Colonization and Globalization* (New York: Routledge, 2002); Lois Parkinson Zamora and Monika Kaup, eds., *Baroque New Worlds: Representation, Transculturation, Counterconquest* (Durham, NC: Duke University Press, 2010).

6. Toi Derricotte, *The Black Notebooks: An Interior Journey* (New York: Norton, 1997), 128.

Chapter 3

1. *Family Worship in a Plantation in S.C.*, appearing in "The War in America: The Federals shelling the City of Charleston—shell bursting in the streets. From a sketch by our special artist," *Illustrated London News*, December 5, 1863, Sacred Arts Collection, Special Collections, Buswell Library, Wheaton College, Wheaton, IL.

2. Robert Knapp, "Coping in Bondage: Slaves," in *Invisible Romans* (Cambridge, MA: Harvard University Press, 2011), 125–69; Peter Garnsey and Richard Saller, *The Roman Empire: Economy, Society, and Culture*, 2nd ed. (Berkeley: University of California Press, 2015), 131–84; Emanuel Mayer, *The Ancient Middle Classes: Urban Life and Aesthetics in the Roman Empire: 100 BCE–250 CE* (Cambridge, MA: Harvard University Press, 2012).

3. Henry Louis Gates Jr., *The Signifying Monkey: A Theory of African-American Criticism* (Oxford: Oxford University Press, 1988), 44–124.

4. Elizabeth Fox-Genovese and Eugene D. Genovese, *The Mind of the*

Master Class: History and Faith in the Southern Slaveholder's Worldview (Cambridge: Cambridge University Press, 2005).

5. Ellis Cose, *The Rage of a Privileged Class* (New York: Harper Perennial, 1993), 48–49.

6. Ned Sublette and Constance Sublette, *The American Slave Coast: A History of the Slave-Breeding Industry* (Chicago: Lawrence Hill Books, 2016).

7. Frederic Jameson, *The Political Unconscious: Narrative as a Socially Symbolic Act* (Ithaca, NY: Cornell University Press, 1981).

8. Interestingly, Rebecca S. Chopp, in her important book *Saving Work: Feminist Practices in Theological Education* (Louisville: Westminster John Knox, 1995), makes a similar observation, drawing on the insight of Elisabeth Schüssler Fiorenza where Schüssler Fiorenza states "that women not only have to move from lay to professional persona but [also] to a masculine, assertive, central speaking public one." Chopp goes on to note the direction of Schüssler Fiorenza's point here: "Women are supposed to master the discourses and disciplines of theological education and assume the subject position of an elite white Eurocentric male. Schüssler Fiorenza observes that women actually have three possibilities. The first possibility is that women can assume the masculine position and learn to do it like a man. The second possibility is that women can totally reject this subject position and try to find preferred 'feminine' ways. . . . A third possibility is for women to become bilingual and learn the male system in order to transform it." She "calls women who follow the third option [of] resident aliens . . . both insider and outsider . . . insider by virtue of residence or patriarchal affiliation to a male citizen or institution; outsider in terms of language, experience, culture and history" (115). I am indebted to Ted Smith for reminding me of this piece of Chopp's text.

9. Thavolia Glymph, *Out of the House of Bondage: The Transformation of the Plantation Household* (Cambridge: Cambridge University Press, 2008).

Chapter 4

1. Willie James Jennings, "Race and the Educated Imagination: Outlining a Pedagogy of Belonging," *Religious Education* 112, no. 1 (2017): 58–65.

2. David Rex Galindo, *To Sin No More: Franciscans and Conversion in the Hispanic World, 1683–1830* (Stanford, CA: Stanford University Press, 2017); Webb Keane, *Christian Moderns: Freedom and Fetish in the Mission Encounter* (Berkeley: University of California Press, 2007), 1–58; Alan Durston, *Pastoral Quechua: The History of Christian Translation in Colonial Peru, 1550–1650*

(Notre Dame: University of Notre Dame Press, 2007); Stuart B. Schwartz, *All Can Be Saved: Religious Tolerance and Salvation in the Iberian Atlantic World* (New Haven: Yale University Press, 2008).

3. Jennings, "Race and the Educated Imagination," 60.

4. Houston A. Baker Jr., *Modernism and the Harlem Renaissance* (Chicago: University of Chicago Press, 1987); Ibram X. Kendi, *Stamped from the Beginning: The Definitive History of Racist Ideas in America* (New York: Nation Books, 2016).

5. Kevin K. Gaines, *Uplifting the Race: Black Leadership, Politics, and Culture in the Twentieth Century* (Chapel Hill: University of North Carolina Press, 1996); Carol Anderson, *Bourgeois Radicals: The NAACP and the Struggle for Colonial Liberation, 1941–1960* (New York: Cambridge University Press, 2015); Joy James, *Transcending the Talented Tenth: Black Leaders and American Intellectuals* (New York: Routledge, 1997).

6. Of course, there are always exceptions to this vision of education, and one of the most important was Howard Thurman, whose vision of the beloved community remains underappreciated and undertheorized or theologized. See his *With Head and Heart: The Autobiography of Howard Thurman* (New York: Harcourt, Brace, 1979); Howard Thurman, *The Search for Common Ground* (Richmond, IN: Friends United Press, 2000); Howard Thurman, *The Creative Encounter: An Interpretation of Religion and the Social Witness* (Richmond, IN: Friends United Press, 1972).

7. Ronald E. Butchart, *Schooling the Freed People: Teaching, Learning, and the Struggle for Black Freedom, 1861–1976* (Chapel Hill: University of North Carolina Press, 2010); Ann Laura Stoler, *Race and the Education of Desire: Foucault's History of Sexuality and the Colonial Order of Things* (Durham, NC: Duke University Press, 1995); Jonathan D. Jansen, *Knowledge in the Blood: Confronting Race and the Apartheid Past* (Stanford, CA: Stanford University Press, 2009); Bradley A. Levinson, Douglas E. Foley, and Dorothy C. Holland, eds., *The Cultural Production of the Educated Person: Critical Ethnographies of Schooling and Local Practice* (Albany: State University of New York Press, 1996).

8. Lisa H. Sideris, *Consecrating Science: Wonder, Knowledge, and the Natural World* (Berkeley: University of California Press, 2017).

Chapter 5

1. Tomoko Masuzawa, *The Invention of World Religions* (Chicago: University of Chicago Press, 2005); Talal Asad, *Genealogies of Religion: Discipline*

and Reasons of Power in Christianity and Islam (Baltimore: Johns Hopkins University Press, 1993); Serge Gruzinski, *The Eagle and the Dragon: Globalization and European Dreams of Conquest in China and America in the Sixteenth Century* (Malden, MA: Polity, 2014); Sudipta Kaviraj, *The Imaginary Institution of India: Politics and Ideas* (New York: Columbia University Press, 2010); David Chidester, *Empire of Religion: Imperialism and Comparative Religion* (Chicago: University of Chicago Press, 2014).

2. Boaventura de Sousa Santos, *The End of the Cognitive Empire: The Coming of Age of Epistemologies of the South* (Durham, NC: Duke University Press, 2018).

3. Winthrop D. Jordan, *The White Man's Burden: The Historical Origins of Racism in the United States* (Oxford: Oxford University Press, 1974); Marilyn Lank and Henry Reynolds, *Drawing the Colour Line: White Men's Countries and the International Challenge of Racial Equality* (Cambridge: Cambridge University Press, 2008); Aileen Moreton Robinson, *The White Possessive: Property, Power, and Indigenous Sovereignty* (Minneapolis: University of Minnesota Press, 2015).

4. Mahmood Mamdani, *When Victims Become Killers: Colonialism, Nativism, and the Genocide in Rwanda* (Princeton: Princeton University Press, 2001); Pekka Hämäläinen, *Comanche Empire* (New Haven: Yale University Press, 2008); Wade Churchill, *Struggle for the Land: Native North American Resistance to Genocide, Ecocide, and Colonization* (San Francisco: City Lights, 2002); David E. Stannard, *American Holocaust: The Conquest of the New World* (New York: Oxford University Press, 1992).

5. Joseph C. Miller, *Way of Death: Merchant Capitalism and the Angolan Slave Trade: 1730–1830* (Madison: University of Wisconsin Press, 1996); Willie James Jennings, *The Christian Imagination: Theology and the Origins of Race* (New Haven: Yale University Press, 2010), 171–80.

6. Randy J. Sparks, *Where the Negroes Are Masters: An African Port in the Era of the Slave Trade* (Cambridge, MA: Harvard University Press, 2014); Robin Law, *Ouidah: The Social History of a West African Slaving Port, 1727–1892* (Oxford: James Currey, 2004).

7. Elizabeth A. Povinelli, *The Empire of Love: Toward a Theory of Intimacy, Genealogy, and Carnality* (Durham, NC: Duke University Press, 2006); Elizabeth A. Povinelli, *Geontologies: A Requiem to Late Liberalism* (Durham, NC: Duke University Press, 2016); Lisbeth Lipari, *Listening, Thinking, Being: Toward an Ethics of Attunement* (University Park: Pennsylvania State University Press, 2014).

8. Starting with the magisterial work of Audre Lorde, "Uses of the Erotic: The Erotic as Power," in *Sister Outsider: Essays and Speeches by Audre Lorde* (Freedom, CA: Crossing, 1984), 53–59; Rita Nakashima Brock, *Journeys by Heart: A Christology of Erotic Power* (Eugene, OR: Wipf & Stock, 2008); Wendy Farley, *The Wounding and Healing of Desire: Weaving Heaven and Earth* (Louisville: Westminster John Knox, 2005), also her *Eros for the Other: Retaining Truth in a Pluralistic World* (University Park: Pennsylvania State University Press, 1996).

9. Lorde, "Uses of the Erotic," 55.

10. Brock, *Journeys by Heart,* 26.

11. Willie James Jennings, *Acts* (Louisville: Westminster John Knox, 2017), 53–61.

12. Farley, *The Wounding and Healing of Desire*, 99.